DSDM

The Agile Software Development Series

Alistair Cockburn and Jim Highsmith, Series Editors
For more information, check out www.awprofessional.com

Agile software development centers on four values identified in the Agile Alliance's Manifesto:

- ◆ Individuals and interactions over processes and tools
- ◆ Working software over comprehensive documentation
- ◆ Customer collaboration over contract negotiation
- ◆ Responding to change over following a plan

The development of Agile software requires innovation and responsiveness, based on generating and sharing knowledge within a development team and with the customer. Agile software developers draw on the strengths of customers, users, and developers, finding just enough process to balance quality and agility.

The books in the **Agile Software Development Series** focus on sharing the experiences of such Agile developers. Individual books address individual techniques (such as Use Cases), group techniques (such as collaborative decision-making), and proven solutions to different problems from a variety of organizational cultures. The result is a core of Agile best practices that will enrich your experience and improve your work.

Titles in the series:

Alistair Cockburn, *Surviving Object-Oriented Projects*, ISBN 0-201-49834-0
Alistair Cockburn, *Writing Effective Use Cases*, ISBN 0-201-70225-8
Alistair Cockburn, *Agile Software Development*, ISBN 0-201-69969-9
Alistair Cockburn, *Agile Software Development Ecosystems*, ISBN 0-201-76043-6
Lars Mathiassen, Jan Pries-Heje and Ojelanki Ngwenyama, *Improving Software Organizations*: *From Principles to Practice*, ISBN 0-201-75820-2
The DSDM Consortium, *DSDM: Business Focused Development* second edition, ISBN 0-321-11224-5

DSDM

Business Focused Development

Second edition

The DSDM Consortium
Edited by
Jennifer Stapleton

consortium

 ADDISON-WESLEY

An imprint of **Pearson Education**

London • Boston • Indianapolis • New York • Mexico City
Toronto • Sydney • Tokyo • Singapore • Hong Kong • Cape Town
New Delhi • Madrid • Paris • Amsterdam • Munich • Milan

PEARSON EDUCATION LIMITED

Edinburgh Gate
Harlow, Essex CM20 2JE
Tel: +44 (0)1279 623623
Fax: +44 (0) 1279 431059
Website: www.pearsoned.co.uk

Coventry University

First published in Great Britain in 1997
Second edition published in Great Britain in 2003

© DSDM Consortium 2003

The right of The DSDM Consortium to be identified as the Authors of this Work has been asserted by them
in accordance with the Copyright, Designs and Patents Act 1988.

ISBN 0-321-11224-5

British Library Cataloguing-in-Publication Data
A CIP catalogue record for this book can be obtained from the British Library

Library of Congress Cataloging-in-Publication Data

Stapleton, Jennifer.
    DSDM : business focussed development / Jennifer Stapleton, with the DSDM
    Consortium.—2nd ed.
        p. cm. — (Agile software development series)
    Includes bibliographical references and index.
    ISBN 0-321-11224-5 (pbk. : alk. paper)
        1. Computer software—Development. 2. System design. I. Title. II. Series.

QA76.76.D47 S7 2003
005.1´1—dc21

2002035733

10 9 8 7 6 5 4

Typeset by Pantek Arts Ltd, Maidstone, Kent.
Printed and bound in Great Britain by Biddles Ltd, King's Lynn, Norfolk

The Publishers' policy is to use paper manufactured from sustainable forests.

Contents at a Glance

Contents

Foreword

It has been five years since Version 1 was published and we have seen quite a change in the Application Development landscape over this period. The turn of the millennium, which to all intents and purposes passed uneventfully, the dot com boom and bust, and in 2002 the worst global recession for a decade. Fads have come and gone, but one thing remains the same; projects are still failing in this millennium for the same reasons as in the last, so the continuation of DSDM (or, as it is now known, the Framework for Business Centred Development) remains necessary and important.

Success in business is about delivering. Delivering to the customer, delivering on time and delivering on budget. This is exactly why DSDM was created: to ensure that quality business systems could be delivered when they were needed. DSDM is a user-centered project delivery framework, which focuses on ensuring on-time delivery of projects that meet business needs. DSDM can be used with a variety of approaches such as eXtreme Programming and Prince2.

The Consortium originated in the United Kingdom in 1994 and there are now consortia worldwide: in the UK, North America, Benelux, Denmark, France, and Sweden. The DSDM Consortium is a not-for-profit membership organization with members varying from blue-chip solutions vendors, to end users, to independent consultants, to academic institutions. Some have been with DSDM from the beginning, others have only recently discovered the benefits of the DSDM approach.

The Framework for Business Centred Development DSDM Version 4.1 was published in 2001. As always with all DSDM products and services this was written by members and is regularly updated in light of member feedback. DSDM is evolving and changing because our members are using it to achieve business goals. As the marketplace changes so does DSDM in its focus and content. DSDM originated out of a need for a better way to develop software and now it is at the forefront of the Agile movement, promoting lightweight methodologies that ensure user involvement and responsiveness to business change. It could be argued that this is what DSDM has always been about and its agility is the reason it still exists in a market where short life spans are a norm.

This book is an overview of what the framework is all about. It is not a replacement for the online manual that members of the consortium use. DSDM is owned by its members and so only members are able to use DSDM commercially. The online manual contains detailed information on all the products, management tools and techniques, and development tools and techniques. Before any attempt to implement DSDM you need to read the online manual and make full use of the resources of the Consortium.

This book is aimed at those involved in delivering IT-focused projects but this does not preclude those from outside IT finding something useful in this overview. In fact as DSDM is about getting users involved, it is expected that anyone involved in a project would benefit from reading more about the DSDM approach.

In Part I you will find an overview of the framework plus some practical examples of how it is implemented. In Part II you will find case studies showing DSDM in action. These cases detail some of the successes and problems encountered when using DSDM. Part III tells you what to do next once you realize DSDM is an approach you could use, with details of where to get more information, how to join the Consortium, and how to get started with DSDM. Finally, in Part IV, you'll find useful appendices.

And finally a thank you to all those people involved in creating this book. As always with DSDM, everything you will read here was written by our members based on their experiences. A particular thank you to Jennifer Stapleton for editing this version as she did Volume 1. Without dedicated members to continue this evolvement, the DSDM consortium would cease to exist and the framework would become obsolete. The framework is user-centered and member driven and through our membership model we aim for it to stay that way. I hope you enjoy the read. I would also encourage you to look at our website www.dsdm.org to see how you can become active in this field.

Barry Fazackerley
DSDM Chairman

Introduction

BACKGROUND

For 40 years the business community has looked to the automation of clerical processes both for efficiency and to gain elusive competitive advantage. In that period, information technology practitioners have consistently failed to deliver the necessary solutions on time, within budget, or to provide the functionality needed by the business.

It has taken us this amount of time to understand that business requirements change rapidly and are difficult to define, and that the people who understand business processes best are the people who use them day-by-day. We have seen that development projects can gain a life of their own, and become enmeshed in their own complexity, but we have learned that applications development is not a black art, and is amenable to structure and discipline.

During the last two decades of the twentieth century, a number of serious attempts have been made to understand the application development process and to codify ways in which these failures can be overcome. In 1994, information systems professionals in the UK from large and small organizations in a wide variety of industries, came together with consultants and project managers from some of the largest companies in the IT industry to form a not-for-profit consortium. This consortium is dedicated to understanding the best practice in application development and codifying it in a way that can be widely taught and implemented.

The result is DSDM (Dynamic Systems Development Method), a project delivery framework that truly serves the need of the business: DSDM projects deliver on time, to budget, and they don't cut important corners. Everything in the published framework has resulted from practical experience and successful application by the membership. This strongly practical approach leads many people to view the framework as being 'just common sense', but it is apparent to anyone trying to control agile developments just how uncommon 'common sense' can be.

Today, the framework is being used on a wide variety of projects, small and large, simple and complex, IT and non-IT, in many countries, and the consortium continues its work to refine the content of the framework. For instance, in June 2001, the consortium issued a version of DSDM specifically aimed at e-business projects where all the reasons for delivering quality systems quickly are possibly even more important. The basic framework underwent a significant update in the summer of 2001 and an incremental improvement was made in January 2002.

Given that we are predominantly building business systems with some IT content, the philosophy behind DSDM is simple:

◆ Development is a team effort. It must combine the customers' knowledge of the business requirements with the technical skills of IT professionals.

◆ High quality demands fitness for purpose as well technical robustness.

◆ Development can be incremental – not everything has to be delivered at once, and delivering something earlier is often more valuable than delivering everything later.

◆ The law of diminishing returns applies – resources must be spent developing the features of most value to the business.

DSDM is about people, not tools. It is about truly understanding the needs of the business and delivering solutions that work – and delivering them as quickly and as cheaply as possible. The framework will not solve every project's problems, but it will go a long way towards ensuring that the business gets the systems it needs in the twenty-first century.

WHAT IS DSDM?

The first questions to ask when coming to DSDM are what is it and why is it different? Despite its full name it is not a method in the accepted sense, but a framework of controls focused on delivering quickly, supplemented by guidance on how to apply those controls. It is a method in as much as it defines a process and a set of products, but these have been deliberately kept at a high level so that they can be tailored for any technical and business environment. There are no prescribed techniques but suggested paths are supplied for implementers of both structured and object-oriented approaches. It is different because it is possibly the only publicly available approach that covers all aspects of system development from the first idea for a project up to the final removal of the project's solution. It addresses the needs of all project participants: business management, project managers, solution architects, solution developers, solution users, and quality assurance personnel.

DSDM describes project management, estimating, prototyping, timeboxing, configuration management, testing, quality assurance, roles and responsibilities (of both users and IT staff), team structures, tool environments, risk management, building for maintainability, reuse and vendor/purchaser relationships – all in a fast-moving, business-centered environment.

The purpose of the framework is to achieve rapid time to market: building what the business needs, when it needs it. If the system is to meet the business needs, then it must be sufficiently robust to be usable in the operational environment. Secondly, the immediate needs of the business can probably be met in the short term and allow for delivery of additional functionality later on.

A BIT OF HISTORY

Businesses are putting increasing pressures on their IT suppliers to deliver better systems, faster and cheaper. In today's rapidly changing world, they are no longer able to wait for years for a system to be provided: the business may have changed radically during the years of development. It is imperative to find a different way of building IT systems. The technology that is now available to developers allows for more speedy production of systems but the answer lies not only in the use of tools. The whole process needs to change. The classical, waterfall lifecycle does not take full advantage of modern technology and does not facilitate the change that is inherent in all systems development. It has been around for about 40 years and is basically the solution to an old problem – that of not having a full understanding of the problem to be solved and not having a coherent approach to solving the problem before starting to code a solution.

The waterfall approach of a strict sequence of stages has been seen to be flawed for many years now. Several attempts have been made to move away from it, including Barry Boehm's iterative style of development using a spiral model of planning, risk analysis, engineering, and customer evaluation. Though excellent, the spiral model did not achieve the penetration into IT practices that it deserved. The emergence in recent years of many 'Agile' methods proves the need for a different approach. While some, such as Extreme Programming, have gained wide acceptance they do not cover all aspects of a project and can leave an organization confused as to how to integrate the many solutions on offer. This provides one explanation for the less than optimal acceptance of agility as the way forward by the majority of IT solution providers. Another could be that, until recently, there has not been sufficient pressure from their customers.

In the early 1990s, the IT industry had become increasingly aware of Rapid Application Development following James Martin's book *Rapid Application Development*, which gave some excellent pointers as to how to make the concept work, but did not provide the total solution. There are many tools on the market, but to use them often meant buying the vendor's process as well. The founding members of the DSDM Consortium saw this as a block to the growth of successful and fast solution delivery.

The Consortium was inaugurated in January 1994 with the aim of producing a public domain, commonly agreed method which would be tool-independent. Ed Holt who chaired the Consortium for the first two years said that every organization that bought a RAD *tool* really needed a new *process*. DSDM aims to provide that process for building and maintaining systems that meet tight time constraints in a controlled project environment. The Consortium had 17 founder members who represented a mix of organizations that remains today: large IT vendors, smaller tool vendors, and user organizations of all sizes. The Consortium now has hundreds of members with established regional consortia in North America, Benelux, Sweden, France, and Denmark with interest growing in other countries, such as Australia, India, and China.

During 1994, the Consortium's Technical Work Group put together the process and produced guidance material based on the experiences and best practices of Consortium members. A few components of the framework were original ideas from experts in particular areas, but most of them were tried and tested – but they had never been brought together as a cohesive approach.

After Version 1 of the framework was published early in 1995, an Early Adopter Programme was put in place to monitor the use of the framework in practice. After feedback from the Early Adopters and the addition of material that had been deliberately left out of Version 1 to get the framework visible as soon as possible, Version 2 was published in November 1995. Following feedback from the wider use of the framework, Version 3 was published in August 1997. Up until 2001 additions to the framework came via UK government White Papers on topics as diverse as using DSDM in data warehousing, component-based development and prototyping business processes. In 2000, it became clear that there was a need for a version of DSDM that was less generic in its definitions and specifically aimed at e-business projects. The technical work of the consortium continues: it is still collecting feedback from users of the framework, and addresses particular needs as they arise through the production of White Papers. A recent White Paper covers the use of UML in DSDM projects.

To ensure that the framework is well understood and applied correctly, a training and examination process was launched alongside Version 1 and continues to evolve. At the time of writing, over 20,000 people have been trained by accredited training providers and increasing numbers are going through the examination process to become certified DSDM Practitioners.

OVERVIEW OF THE FRAMEWORK

The whole framework is based on nine principles, which are discussed in more detail later on, but it is useful to list them here. The first four define the foundations on which DSDM is built and the other five provide the principles that have guided the structure of the framework.

1. Active user involvement is imperative.

2. DSDM teams must be empowered to make decisions.

3. The focus is on frequent delivery of products.

4. Fitness for business purpose is the essential criterion for acceptance of deliverables.

5. Iterative and incremental development is necessary to converge on an accurate business solution.

6. All changes during development are reversible.

7. Requirements are baselined at a high level.

8. Testing is integrated throughout the lifecycle.

9. A collaborative and co-operative approach between all stakeholders is essential.

All of these principles have been found to be necessary, if a quality system is to be supplied in the timescales required by the business.

The iterative and incremental process embodied in the fifth principle consists of five development phases. (There are two non-development phases: *pre-project*, which ensures that the project is set up on a sound basis, and *post-project*, which includes keeping the delivered solution operational.) The first two development phases are sequential: *feasibility* to assess the suitability of the system to the approach and to provide an initial view of the costs, etc., followed by the *business study* which builds the business and technical foundations of the rest of the project. After the business study, the first of the iterative phases is the *functional model iteration* in which the analysis started in the business study is done in more detail. The analysis is supported by evolutionary prototyping of functionality inside the system architecture that is also defined at a high level in the business study. When an area of functionality is well enough understood, the *design and build iteration* engineers the system component to sufficient quality to be delivered in the *implementation* phase. Implementation covers not only moving the system to the production environment but also training the users. At the end of implementation, the increment is reviewed and a business decision is made about what further work (if any) needs to be done in subsequent increments.

No process is complete without the people to enact it. The first principle states that the solution's users must be closely involved throughout development: their regular input and feedback are essential to the framework. DSDM defines roles for the people involved in a DSDM project. These include both users and development staff. For example, one user role is that of Visionary. This is usually taken by the person who is responsible for getting the project started through their vision for IT support in the business area. A key IT role is that of Technical Co-ordinator, who is basically the system architect and keeper of the technical vision. The combination of these two roles ensures the business and technical foundations of the project are secure, but there are many more roles defined in both areas of specialism.

The aim of DSDM is to deliver systems to timescales that would be impossible using the waterfall approach. The impact is that the work processes have to be managed in a different way and the techniques used within those processes need to be honed down to reduce overheads as much as possible. The major instrument for controlling work is the timebox. The timebox in DSDM is a short period of time (a matter of days or a few weeks) within a project when something is produced to defined quality objectives, so satisfying the third, fourth, and eighth principles. By taking a product-based view rather than an activity-based view of process, DSDM allows the controls to be focused on what is produced rather than the method of production. This enables a flexible approach to be taken to the techniques used within the framework.

Application of the sixth principle of reversible change means that everything that is produced must be controlled sufficiently well in order to move back to a known state when any product proves to be wrong.

So DSDM is about controlling a style of development that is often viewed as a way of producing unmaintainable systems. It keeps a firm focus on satisfying the business needs rather than IT's perception of them. The application of DSDM's user-centered, iterative, and incremental approach results in many benefits. As has been proven on thousands of projects, these include:

- the users are more likely to take ownership of the system;
- the risk of building the wrong system is reduced;
- the final system is more likely to meet the users' real business requirements;

♦ the users will be better trained;

♦ the system implementation is more likely to go more smoothly.

WHY IS DSDM MORE RAPID THAN THE WATERFALL?

DSDM produces 'industrial strength' systems that meet users' needs and are fully extendible and maintainable over long periods of time – they are not one-off or throwaway. In business terms, they are the exact peer of good systems developed by the waterfall approach, but take a lot less time to develop.

There are two main reasons. Less is actually done. There is much less time spent in briefing people, and bringing them repeatedly up to speed. Little time is lost through task-switching by users or developers. Most importantly of all, only the features that are needed are actually developed.

The second reason is that problems, misunderstandings and false directions are identified and corrected early, so avoiding the massive rewrites often required late in waterfall projects. This has a further benefit. The resultant code developed under DSDM is consistent and of a piece, whereas waterfall code, by the end of the project, is often already patched and out of synchrony with its documentation. The result is that DSDM-delivered code is also easier to maintain.

ABOUT THIS BOOK

While the online manual is obviously the first port of call when the framework needs to be understood in depth, it is necessarily focused on what the framework contains rather than stories and comments on how the framework has been used in varying environments. The first edition of *DSDM: The Method in Practice* was commissioned by the DSDM Consortium to provide a practical rather than theoretical view of the framework. It is now out of date since both the framework and the world in which the framework is used have moved on. Alongside the evolution of the framework, organizations are using it for many more types of project than it was originally designed, from business process change programs to advertising campaigns. This book will focus on application development projects but one case study shows the use of DSDM in a non-IT program.

Part I offers an overview of the framework as described in the online manual but more importantly it contains anecdotes and information from real projects. Part II contains some case studies that have been provided by participants in the projects described. They cover what their authors felt were important aspects of their projects. They are definitely a miscellany, being of varying lengths and of varying depth of description, but we hope that you will find something of value in each one. Part III provides information about how to contact the consortium, how to become a member, and how to access the resources of the consortium. In Part IV you can read about the birth of the Agile manifesto and find out where to go next.

ABOUT THE AGILE SOFTWARE DEVELOPMENT SERIES

The Agile Software Development series highlights effective light, human-powered development techniques, based on two core ideas:

- Different projects need different processes or methodologies.

- Focusing on skills, communication, and community allows the project to be more agile and effective than focusing on processes.

Two books anchor the Agile Software Development series:

- *Agile Software Development* (Cockburn, 2002) describes the economic and psychological principles underlying agile development. It introduces two ideas, that a methodology is the set of conventions a development team agrees to adopt, and that systems and software development is fruitfully viewed as a resource-constrained co-operative game of invention and communication. From those views and principles, practitioners can select and personalize an agile approach for their local situation.

- *Agile Software Development Ecosystems* (Cockburn, 2002) describes the people behind the Agile Software Development Manifesto (http://agilemanifesto.org), the methodologies they developed, and experiences in using agile techniques.

The series has three tracks:

- Techniques to improve the effectiveness of a person who is doing a particular sort of job. This might be a person who is designing a user interface, gathering requirements, planning a project, designing, or testing. Whoever is performing such a job will want to know how the best people in the world do their jobs. *Writing Effective Use Cases* (Cockburn, 2001), *Configuration Management Principles and Practices* (Hass, 2002), and *GUIs with Glue* (Hohmann, in preparation) are technique books.

- Techniques to improve the effectiveness of a group of people. These might include techniques for team-building, project retrospectives, decision-making, or running effective meetings. *Improving Software Organizations* (Mathiassen,

2001) and *Surviving Object-Oriented Projects* (Cockburn 1998) are two group technique books.

◆ Examples of successful methodologies. Whoever is selecting a methodology will want to find one that has been successfully used in a similar situation. Personalizing that methodology will be easier than creating a new one from scratch and is more effective than using one that was designed for a different situation. This DSDM book and *Crystal Clear* (Cockburn, in preparation) are descriptions of tried methodologies.

You can find resources about DSDM and agile development on the Web. Specific sites and topics are included in the References at the back. A starter set includes these sites:

◆ www.DSDM.org is the home site for the DSDM Consortium, with news and leads to other resources.

◆ www.AgileAlliance.org describes the activities of the non-profit organization the AgileAlliance, and has links to agile development discussion groups around the world.

◆ www.Alistair.Cockburn.us/crystal holds a growing library of papers, sample work products and agile processes, and a discussion area for agile development topics.

PART I

The Framework

Chapter 1

DSDM Process Overview

1.1 INTRODUCTION

Figure 1.1 shows the development process. This is affectionately known as 'the three pizzas and a cheese'. As stated in the introduction, the DSDM development lifecycle has five phases. The forward path follows the dark arrows, and recognized routes back to evolve the system are shown by the lighter arrows. As stated in the Introduction, the DSDM lifecycle has seven phases. These are:

1. pre-project;

2. feasibility study;

3. business study;

4. functional model iteration;

5. system design and build iteration;

6. implementation;

7. post-project.

The pre-project phase ensures that only the right projects are started and that they are set up correctly. Once it has been determined that a project is to go ahead, funding is available, etc., the initial project planning for the feasibility study is done. Then the project proper begins with the feasibility study.

The feasibility and business studies are done sequentially. They set the ground rules for the rest of development, which is iterative and incremental, and therefore they must be completed before any further work is carried out on a given project. How the latter three phases overlap and merge is left to a particular project to

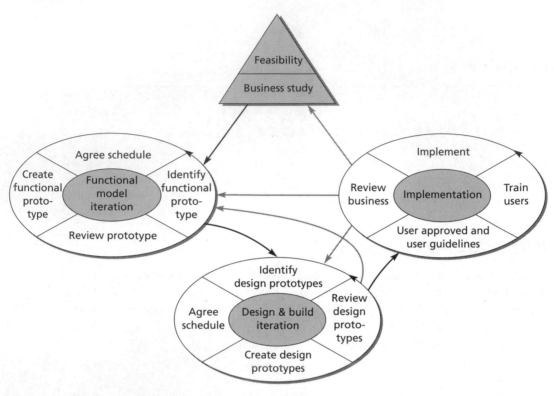

Figure 1.1 *DSDM process diagram*

decide. A project team may decide to do all the functional model iterations before moving on to system design and build iterations and finally iterating through the placement of the system in the working environment. However, this approach effectively is just iterating inside the stages of a waterfall lifecycle and does not take full advantage of the flexibility that DSDM offers. Before looking at the various ways that projects have used the latter three phases, we need to understand what the overall aims of the phases are and the products that are derived in each phase.

Each of the products mentioned in this chapter is considered essential to the success of a DSDM project, but the way in which they are produced and their detailed content is left to be defined in organizational standards or on a project-by-project basis. The DSDM Consortium has taken the view that to include all possible products in all possible projects could lead to slavish following of an over-engineered lifecycle. This minimum set of products can be expanded but should never be reduced without good reason. Some additional products may be needed for every project in an organization depending on local practices, but the framework should be tried out on several projects before this is done to ensure that the process is not being unnecessarily overloaded.

Some method developers have taken the opposite view to that of the DSDM Consortium and tried to cater for every possibility and as a result have gained a name for being too lengthy in their application. Although this is a fault in the application of such methods rather than their contents, it would be disastrous for an agile method to become known as bureaucratic or over-complex. DSDM hopes that, by taking a minimalist approach, careful thought will be given to the nature of each project and its inherent risks. The result should be a product set that is suited to the needs of the project under consideration.

In line with this minimalist approach, the DSDM online manual defines each phase of the process in terms of its purpose, preconditions, products and the roles involved. It does not supply a particular set of activities within each phase, as this will depend on the application being built, the organization building it, and the organization for whom it is being built. Similarly, products are defined in terms of their purpose and the generic quality criteria by which the products should be assessed. The actual contents will be determined by local practices such as the preferred analysis or project management techniques.

1.2 THE FEASIBILITY STUDY

This phase is more an assessment of whether or not the DSDM approach is the right one for the project than a traditional feasibility study. This is largely because for many feasibility studies, the waterfall approach is implicitly accepted as the default approach to development. When DSDM is offered as an alternative approach by the IT solution supplier (whether internal or external to the organization), then care should be taken that it is indeed appropriate.

The normal considerations in a feasibility study are still present such as a definition of the problem to be addressed together with the answers to questions like 'Do we think the proposed system is technically possible?', 'Is the impact on the current business processes acceptable?' and the bottom line 'Is it worth doing?', but we also have to answer the question 'Is DSDM the best way to build the system?' Some applications will be difficult to produce using DSDM, and other chapters in this book show how to decide what is and what is not amenable to DSDM. The considerations that drive this are organizational and people issues more often than not. To document any problems arising from these questions, the project's risk log is opened now and used in the standard way throughout the project.

First and foremost there is significant impact on the user community if the process is going to work successfully. This impact will be unacceptable to many senior managers unless there is a real business need to deliver the system within timescales that would be considered next to impossible using other methods.

Given that DSDM is to be used for the development of systems that are urgently needed, the feasibility study is necessarily a short, sharp exercise. Some organizations are so cautious in the run-up to development that feasibility studies can take as long as two years before it is finally agreed by all parties that all the ins and outs of the problem have been considered. The DSDM feasibility study will last no more than a few weeks. Therefore the feasibility report will cover all the usual topics but not in great detail. If any areas are considered to be very risky, the decision has to be made as to whether or not to proceed, so there should be sufficient information to make decisions about managing that risk. The key word here is 'sufficient'. The DSDM philosophy is to do enough and no more.

As well as the feasibility report, there are two other products from the feasibility study. Both are produced to support the findings in the feasibility report. The first is an outline plan for development, which will add weight to the findings that desired outcome is achievable, and the second is a fast prototype. The prototype is an optional product. Many projects will have no need to create a feasibility prototype. Its aim is to show that the project is technically feasible, but a key question to ask is 'Does the production of a prototype add value to the contents of the feasibility report?' In many cases the answer will be 'No', because the business is reasonably well understood and the technology is tried and tested within the organization. Even when either of these is not true, it is often wise not to leap into building something before the system is a little better understood. This can engender just the sort of attitude to rapid development that DSDM is designed to negate, i.e. 'Let's build it now and not worry about the consequences six months or a year down the line.'

1.3 THE BUSINESS STUDY

Having decided that DSDM is indeed the way to go, the business study provides the foundations on which all subsequent work is based, but again this is a short exercise to achieve enough understanding of the business and technical constraints to move forward with safety. As its name suggests, the prime activity here is to get a good understanding of the business processes to be automated and their information needs. To achieve this in the short timescales of a DSDM project, this activity is very strongly collaborative. The 'usual' approach to the early stages of analysis by interviewing people separately just will not work. What is needed is a series of facilitated workshops of knowledgeable staff who can quickly pool their knowledge and gain consensus as to the priorities of the development. The result of these workshops will be the Business Area Definition, which will not only identify the business processes and associated information, but also the classes of users who will be affected in any way by the introduction of the system. From these user classes, the individuals who will participate in the development will be identified and agreement reached with their management as to their involvement.

The Business Area Definition is a high-level view of the processes to be automated. In a structured analysis environment, it will probably contain a data flow diagram showing the major processes, but without lower-level refinements of those processes (these will be produced later) and a first pass entity relationship diagram. In an object-oriented environment, it will probably contain a first pass business object model with important Use Cases defined in outline. However, these are only suggestions to give a flavor of the level of detail that is expected in the Business Area Definition. They are not prescribed.

Each of the high-level functions identified in the Business Area Definition and associated non-functional requirements has to be prioritized so that the most important functionality will be developed in preference to less essential parts which can be added on later if required. The prioritization will principally be led by business need, but should also take into account the technical constraints which may drive some functionality to be developed first even though it is less important in business terms.

Because parts of the software will begin to be produced in the next phase (the functional model iteration), it is not only important to understand the functionality to be developed but also the system architecture that will be used. So another product from the business study is the System Architecture Definition, which describes the development and target platforms as well as the architecture of the software to be developed in terms of its major components and their interfaces. As with everything else produced during the business study, the System Architecture Definition is allowed to change during later work. For instance, the first cut placement of processes in a client/server-based system could change due to considerations about network traffic when this is better understood. Moreover, the detail of the system design will be added and refined as work progresses.

Last but not least, the Outline Plan produced as part of the feasibility phase is refined to produce the Development Plan. This covers all prototyping activities in both the functional model iteration and the design and build iteration. It should include not only the prototyping strategy, but also the testing strategy and the configuration management plan. Configuration management assumes great importance in an iterative and incremental approach such as that adopted by DSDM.

1.4 FUNCTIONAL MODEL ITERATION

The focus of the functional model iteration is on refining the business aspects of the system, i.e. building on the high-level functional and information requirements identified during the business study. To this end, both standard analysis models and software are produced. Both the functional model iteration and the design and build iteration consist of cycles of four activities:

1. identify what you are doing in the cycle;

2. agree how you are going to go about it;

3. do it;

4. check that you did it right (by reviewing documents, demonstrating a prototype, or proving that a part of the software has been successfully tested).

The Functional Model which is built up in these cycles consists both of analysis models and of software components which contain the major functionality and will satisfy some of the non-functional requirements, in particular any related to usability. The software components and analysis models are built side by side with the analysis models taking the lead initially. As the cycles continue, the findings of prototyping activities feed back into the analysis models and, as the models are refined, the prototypes are progressively moved towards software which could possibly be delivered, but which is perhaps not as well engineered as it might be in some respects. For instance, although performance considerations should never be left until late in the development, the performance of these early software components could be less than optimal as long as it is known how this will be addressed later.

The symbiotic development of analysis models and functioning software components is not as chaotic as it may at first appear. Later chapters will explain how it is controlled. Unfortunately, some projects claiming to use DSDM ignore this important fact and end up doing analysis on the fly, even though there is specific guidance in the framework on what sort of modeling activities take place. Careful analysis is necessary if the system is to be well-founded.

It is essential that the software components of the Functional Model are tested as they are produced. This obviously includes unit testing but as many other classes of testing that are possible should be undertaken. The focus of testing in the Functional Model will necessarily be on what the components do and whether or not they knit together into a usable set of functionality. Non-functional aspects are tested in the design and build iteration. This gives rise to the backwards arrow in the process diagram from the design and build iteration phase to the functional model iteration. It will often be easier, and indeed more sensible, to address the detail of an area of functionality together with its non-functional aspects in one chunk before addressing the detail of another area. The extent to which the two phases merge will depend largely on how the application breaks down into components and the facilities of the development environment.

Other products that result from the functional model iteration at different stages of its progress are:

- **Prioritized functions:** as analysis proceeds, the detail of the high-level functions identified in the Business Area Definition is produced. Therefore the crude prioritization which took place at that stage is progressively refined during the functional model iteration. It is this refined set of prioritized functions which defines the core functionality which is guaranteed to be delivered to the users at the end of the current increment.

- **Functional prototyping review documents:** as the system is iteratively reviewed by the users, the comments of reviews need to be kept. It is just as important to know what was liked and should therefore be retained as well as what was wrong and needs to be changed or discarded. Obviously the review at the end of one cycle will directly lead into deciding what is to happen in the next cycle, but the review documents can be used across a wider area, even to provide useful information to later projects.

- **Non-functional requirements:** all the non-functional requirements that are elicited during the business study and the functional model iteration should be recorded. Some of these will be satisfied during the functional model iteration, but the majority of them are likely to be dealt with in the design and build iteration. These requirements will focus the activities of the design and build iteration correctly as the development moves away from analysis to more technical issues.

- **Implementation Plan:** as the final cycles through the functional model iteration occur, the business and technical scope of the solution to be delivered by the current increment is consolidated and it becomes clear what activities will be needed to deliver the solution into operation. The Implementation Plan is produced now rather than later in the design and build iteration, so that the knowledge and skills needed to implement the solution will be ready. To delay creating the Implementation Plan will often lead to task scheduling conflicts and endanger the promises made about the delivery date for the increment.

1.5 DESIGN AND BUILD ITERATION

The design and build iteration is where the system is engineered to a sufficiently high standard to be safely placed in the hands of the users. The major product here is obviously the Tested System. The diagram of the DSDM process does not show testing as a distinct activity for the simple reason that testing is happening throughout both the functional model iteration and the design and build iteration. Some environments or contractual arrangements will require separate testing phases to be included at the end of the development of the increment, but this should not be the major activity encountered in the waterfall lifecycle. Testing is just as important in DSDM and has just as much effort involved in it, but it is thinly spread throughout development.

The Tested System will not necessarily satisfy all the requirements identified during development, but it will satisfy all the requirements that have been agreed. The core of requirements (what DSDM calls the minimum usable subset) will of course be contained in the Tested System, with as many other parts of the whole picture added in as time allows.

Intermediate products that come early in the design and build iteration are design prototypes and their associated design prototyping review documents. Design prototypes are intended to be evolutionary, as are the functional prototypes.

1.6 IMPLEMENTATION

The implementation phase covers the cutover from the development environment to the operational environment. This includes training the users and handing over the system to them. This could be as simple as placing the new system on a single PC or as complex as a major system rollout across national boundaries. The iteration in the implementation phase is applicable when the system is being handed over to a dispersed user population over a period of time. Otherwise the phase just iterates once!

The products of this phase obviously include the delivered system, which contains all the necessary documentation. The other components that make the system usable are also included: the User Documentation and a trained user population, where users are taken not only to be the end-users but those people who will support the operation of the solution. The User Documentation is completed in this phase but should have been started earlier. Many projects have found it useful to have the user members of the team produce the user materials while the developers are focused on more technical aspects of development. This is possible since the users in the team understand the system, but the great advantage is that they will be able to describe how to operate it in language that the rest of the user population will understand. This can be a first for some developers.

The other product of this phase is the Increment Review Document. This is produced immediately the system or system increment is deemed complete and does not replace other project review documents produced, say, six months into the operational life of the system where other matters are considered, such as whether or not business benefits have been achieved by the installation of the system. The Increment Review Document is used to summarize what the project has achieved in terms of its short-term objectives. In particular, it reviews the requirements that have been identified during development and assesses the position of the system in relation to those requirements. There are four possible outcomes (three of which are shown by returning arrows on the DSDM process diagram in Figure 1.1). The four outcomes are:

1. All requirements have been satisfied and there is no further work currently envisaged (hence no return arrow!).

2. A major area of business functionality was discovered during development, which had to be temporarily sidelined in order to deliver on the required date. This means returning to the business study and scoping another tranche of development from start to finish.

3. Lower priority functionality was squeezed out of development owing to the timescales and will now be added in. This involves returning to the functional model iteration and working through the process from that point.

4. An area of concern in the design and build iteration was omitted, again owing to time pressure, but can now be addressed. This last point does not mean that a poorly built system was delivered, but that lower priority non-functional aspects have been omitted. For instance, a system may be delivered with a simplified access control which will suffice in the short term, but should be refined for long-term use, or perhaps a non-critical area of the system has been delivered with less than optimal performance characteristics. It could have been decided that the latter was acceptable in the short term but, as volumes of traffic increase with system usage, good performance will become increasingly important.

1.7 POST-PROJECT

Once the solution has been delivered, DSDM moves into the post-project phase. During development, system change requests will often be treated as new requirements and handled by the development team. Once the development team has disbanded, requested changes to the solution are delivered using a DSDM-based process of prioritizing changes, updating the existing solution, and delivering new system releases.

A post-implementation review may be carried out at a time agreed during the project to assess the success of the solution in achieving the intended benefits. Such a review will not usually consider lessons learned during the project, as these will have been considered during the increment reviews.

1.8 KEY POINTS

- The DSDM process provides a framework that should be populated according to organizational practices and project needs.

- The pre-project phase ensures that the project is set up correctly.

- The feasibility study investigates whether or not DSDM is the right approach for the project.

- The business study provides the business and technical foundations for all later development.

- The functional model iteration cycles produce both analysis documentation and working software.

- The design and build iteration engineers the system to the required level for operational use.

- After placing the system in the operational environment during the implementation phase, the scope of what has been delivered and what needs to be delivered next must be assessed.

- The post-project phase uses a variant of DSDM for maintenance activities and reviews the solution in use.

- Testing is performed throughout the iterative phases and is not a discrete activity at the end of the development lifecycle.

- The DSDM products are defined in outline only to allow them to be used in any technical or business environment.

- The set of products is as minimal as it can be, while ensuring safe progress towards delivery and maintenance.

Chapter 2

The Underlying Principles

The foundations of DSDM are contained in nine underlying principles. For DSDM to be successful, all of these principles must be applied in a project. If one of them is ignored, the whole basis of DSDM is endangered. Some projects may find that one or more of the principles is difficult to apply, in which case the use of DSDM should be seriously reconsidered. At the very least, an approach to mitigating the consequence of non-conformance to the principles needs to be thought out.

Each principle has an important place in the way DSDM operates. We will consider them one by one.

Principle 1: Active User Involvement is Imperative

Although the order of the principles has no special significance, this principle deserves its position at the head of the list because it is the most important. The user involvement in a DSDM project is not only active: it is pro-active. In many other approaches to system development, the users are involved at the beginning when requirements are elicited, then sporadically throughout the development work as products such as functional specifications are produced for them to review until they come back in full swing to do the acceptance testing.

The 'normal' user resource curve resembles the cross-section of a rather uncomfortable sofa with large arms and spikes along the seat, as shown in Figure 2.1.

In DSDM the user resource curve is much flatter. If you drew a resource curve for users in a DSDM project, it would be very close to a straight line from near the start of the project to its completion, with smaller spikes when opinions are sought in workshops, demonstrations, etc., and the curve would be much further down the scale. The process involves a few knowledgeable users who support or participate in a development team throughout the project. This is as opposed to the traditional approach of sending out documents to a mass of users for their comments and calling in a fairly large user population for acceptance testing at the end of the process.

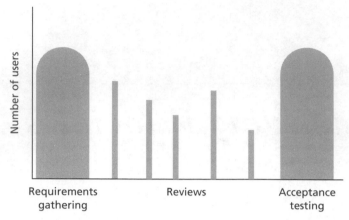

Figure 2.1 *The spiky sofa curve*

The gaps between document reviews using this approach can lead to users losing sight of the aims and progress of the development. This often leads to comments such as 'There is a spelling mistake on page 135', rather than a critique of the content which is what is needed.

Experience has shown that the total effort in a DSDM project from the user community is probably not much greater and is often the same or less. However it is continuous and can therefore be more focused on the needs of the project. Moreover, because the user involvement is present over a much shorter time frame, it can feel much more to both the users themselves and the developers that they are working with.

Having business knowledge available at all times shortens the communication lines between the customers and suppliers of IT systems and enables work to progress much more smoothly. All too often, developers can make false assumptions about what is required on the basis of what they have understood to be true during the early stages of the project. It is this that leads to the unfortunately common scenario of users rejecting work during acceptance testing because it doesn't do 'what they asked for'. It is difficult for users to envisage all that they actually want. It is even harder for them to communicate their requirements to developers who, by the very nature of their work and expertise, cannot have the in-depth understanding of the business that they are trying to support.

The users should be senior enough to have an overall view of the aims of the system under development, but also have detailed knowledge of what constitutes the business processes and what information is needed to support the business processes. Such users are usually important staff in their business area. This can create problems for the normal running of the business. Practical examples of how this can be handled are given in Chapter 7.

Principle 2: DSDM Teams Must be Empowered to Make Decisions

In order for development to move forward quickly, the team members must be able to make quick decisions about the direction that they are taking. DSDM projects are necessarily working to tight timescales and long decision processes that move slowly up and down the hierarchy of management will reduce the chances of delivering what is needed on time. Moreover, there is very little point in having users in the development team if they are unable to make day-to-day decisions about what the system should do. Many DSDM projects have taken this aspect of empowerment to heart and made it work well. However, empowerment also applies to the IT members of the team.

Many managers (both business and IT) worry that they will lose control of the project, but empowerment does not mean 'carte blanche' for staff to do as they wish. They should be given clear guidelines about where the limits lie. Of course, a major constraint on their powers is the budget for the project and no DSDM team should be allowed to move outside that without recourse to more senior management. DSDM supplies a structure for escalating decisions. This includes a list of the sorts of issues that need to be escalated promptly from a team to the project, especially any factors affecting their ability to deliver what is required of them to the expected quality. It also covers the sorts of issues that require escalation from the project to the project's governing body, such as the agreed level of business participation not being achieved.

Frequent small decisions can and should be made by the team. These will include:

- what the requirements mean in practice;

- whether or not the interim products of development are acceptable in terms of functionality, usability, etc.;

- the prioritization of requirements as work progresses;

- altering the fine detail of the technical solution.

None of these will have catastrophic effects on the development. Indeed by placing such decision-making within the team, the team members will recognize more easily what decisions must be made by other people.

It is essential not to restrict the level of empowerment so much that the team make assumptions about what to do. This can only result in the wrong assumptions being made sometimes, leading to wasted time and effort, which are at a premium in a DSDM project.

Principle 3: The Focus is on Frequent Delivery of Products

Some organizations have taken 'products' to mean operational systems, i.e. getting something out to the business in a few months as opposed to a year or so. This is not at all what the principle is about. It covers two important aspects of DSDM projects: controlling activity and working effectively in short timescales.

By requiring frequent delivery of products, the decision-making within the team can be verified as acceptable by staff outside the team. This provides the control that some managers feel that they would otherwise lose over the direction that the project is taking. By having frequent delivery (say every week) of something tangible and visible, the safety net for capturing erroneous decisions and assumptions early is firmly in place.

Products are not just software, but also other key components of development, such as a data model, or a part of it. Products are just something that the team has produced as a step towards delivery of the system. More importantly, a product does not need to be complete as long as it demonstrates progress and can be a basis for checking that the project is going in the right direction.

This emphasis on a product-based approach to managing projects is more flexible than a task-based one. The team members are given a fixed period of time in which to produce something which is clearly defined in terms of purpose and overall content together with criteria by which it will be assessed. How they actually create the product is left to them. For instance, they might be given two weeks to build and integrate a functional area of the system. The team members (users and developers together) then decide what activities are necessary and sufficient to deliver that piece of software to the expected quality. Compare this with the usual approach of assigning low-level tasks to individual team members. In this case, the team cannot easily change the tasks to meet the deadline. If an owner of a task hits some difficulty, the other team members are focused on their own assignments and are unable to reallocate resources to achieve the common goal.

Principle 4: Fitness for Business Purpose is the Essential Criterion for Acceptance of Deliverables

This principle can be reworded as 'Build the right product before you build it right'. Indeed, in Version 1 of DSDM, this is what it said. However, these words were taken to mean that hacking the system together was acceptable. This is absolutely not the case: what the principle means is that the developers should not get bogged down in delivering 'gold-plated' solutions.

By focusing on fitness for business purpose, some technical issues can be left until later if the operational characteristics are sufficiently robust in the short term.

However, some technical issues will directly affect the fitness for business purpose. For instance, if an application is to be used by a call center taking orders, the response times must be excellent.

Traditionally the focus of developers has been on satisfying all the requirements in a requirements document. It may well be that the requirements are inaccurate or actually unnecessary. For instance, the requirements for the call center application may contain a blanket requirement for rapid response times. Certainly, these will be needed for the day-to-day use of the core functionality, but the need for rapid response should be questioned for the housekeeping activities in the system if trying to achieve them will endanger the timescales. These response times can be improved after the system has been installed without affecting its fitness for business purpose at the time of delivery.

Additionally, this principle focuses the quality assurance activities during development. The application of principle three about delivering products frequently should not drown the project in excessive checks that are not based on delivering to the business. Using fitness for business purpose as the basis for checking deliverables means that validation is probably more important than verification. In other words, looking forward to the system in use is better than checking backwards for consistency. All too often in software development, consistency with earlier products which may themselves be flawed in some way becomes the driver for acceptance of an interim product. This can lead to an inflexible approach to deciding what is going to be delivered in the end. In time-constrained projects, maximizing the business benefit has to be the focus of attention at all times.

Principle 5: Iterative and Incremental Development is Necessary to Converge on an Accurate Business Solution

With users in the team providing almost instant feedback on the work of the developers, it is possible for systems to evolve rather than take a one-pass approach to production of working software. By letting systems evolve, DSDM ensures that errors are trapped early before they become costly to correct. Moreover, 'instant', if partial, solutions to business problems can be placed in the workplace while less critical components are developed.

Even before any increment is delivered, iteration is a fact of life – as in all system development. The project manager who has never had to cope with rework of previously 'completed' products is a very lucky person indeed. When rework is not accepted as part of the development process, all signed-off work is treated as sacrosanct and protected from change. This leads to lengthy and often confrontational procedures when earlier work needs to be changed. By recognizing that rework is going to happen and using an iterative process, DSDM allows developers to progress more rapidly towards the production of a system that meets the needs of the business.

The application of this principle is largely possible through the technology that is available to developers today compared with a few decades ago. This can be compared with the different technology available to military air forces. In the past, they loaded slow and cumbersome aircraft with as many bombs as possible. These would be dropped on a target that they could not guarantee to hit – particularly if the target moved. Nowadays, one more effective missile can be launched, it can adjust its course, and can be guaranteed to hit a moving target. In the waterfall approach, we fill up the requirements specification with as many things as might be needed and hope that the correct system will be achieved – even though the business needs may change during development. In DSDM, we can use the technology and the knowledge of the business to make course corrections as we go. The result is less effort for a better targeted system.

Principle 6: All Changes During Development are Reversible

In an iterative and incremental process, it must be possible sometimes to accept that the wrong path has been taken and therefore to backtrack to a known safe point in development. This means that the management of all software components and their associated documents must be excellent. The DSDM online manual provides guidance on how this can be achieved.

Many people on first encountering this principle are worried that it means that large amounts of work will be discarded. This would present a serious problem if, say, the work of the past month were deemed unfit for purpose and the project only lasted three months. However, if the other principles are applied successfully, this should not happen. In particular, the third principle of frequent delivery of products that are visible and checkable will ensure that only recent work needs to be rethought.

Principle 7: Requirements are Baselined at a High Level

The application of this principle within the DSDM lifecycle means that the requirements, which have been captured during the business study, are the agreed high-level scope of the project. By baselining (or 'freezing') requirements at this point, the detailed requirements can be elicited through the iterative process that follows. Of course further baselines can be set later in the process – and indeed they should be – to ensure that work is always based on common understanding of what is required.

If requirements are not baselined before every detail has been considered then prototyping activities will not be directed by the requirements, as they should be, and development can easily run out of control. Another possible outcome of not baselining early is that no software components are allowed to be produced before all the requirements have been established. This means that the users will be unable to visualize the impact of their requirements until later in the lifecycle – a return to one of the problems that DSDM is designed to alleviate.

Principle 8: Testing is Integrated Throughout the Lifecycle

DSDM does not subscribe to the opinion of some methods that testing is done after the more creative parts of development. This is too late and potentially disastrous. It often leads to testing being at best cursory and at worst ignored entirely due to time constraints. Such practice is one of the contributing factors to agile methods being thought of as 'quick and dirty'.

Since partial system components are produced very early on in the life of a DSDM project and evolve into the delivered system, the philosophy of DSDM is to 'test as you go'. As developers produce a software component, it is tested by themselves (for technical aspects) and the users in the team (for functional suitability). In this way, all forms of testing, including acceptance testing, are carried out incrementally throughout a project. Integration testing is performed as soon as there is something to integrate and evolutionary development means that regression testing is very important in DSDM. Building something new that does not fit with previous components or damages the way they work should not be allowed to happen.

By demanding testing throughout development, DSDM projects can continuously demonstrate the quality of what they are producing, so enabling IT management and business management to be confident that the system will be fit for purpose from their respective points of view.

Principle 9: A Collaborative and Co-operative Approach Between all Stakeholders is Essential

One organization tried to remove this principle from its application of DSDM because it found it too problematical, particularly when it was contracting work to external software suppliers. The projects quickly returned to the 'us and them' attitudes that are counter to the DSDM process in which responsibilities are shared. Developers cannot divine what is needed without support from the end-users.

The key words here are not only that collaboration and co-operation are important, but also that all stakeholders need to buy in to the approach. This means that not only must the user/developer relationships be made to work effectively, but also that different parts of the business and IT organizations must also co-operate.

Some organizations put up artificial barriers between different parts of the IT department. It is useless for the application development staff to put a system together quickly if the operational staff do not view its take-on as important and delay it due to their own conflicting set of priorities.

IT departments are not the only culprits. A system may easily have some impact on the workings of a business area that is viewed as peripheral by the main users of the system. If their interests are not taken into account early, the whole process can founder. For instance, a large bank used DSDM to build some essential new systems without informing their financial auditors of the changes that were being made to the development process. The auditors expected certain documents to be produced during development, so that they could check the validity of the work. These documents were not present and the auditors almost came to the point of demanding that the systems be taken out of use until they were present. However, once they understood the different controls in DSDM, they were satisfied that all was well, and a major problem was averted.

This principle also has an impact when software is being built by an external supplier. Contractual arguments about what should and should not be delivered are counter-productive. Moreover, many organizations have procurement departments who provide the principal contact with the suppliers. When the purchasing organization places such barriers between the end-users and the suppliers, DSDM will not work at all. Many external suppliers are using DSDM: it can work, but there has to be trust on both sides – purchaser and supplier. A skeleton contract, based on UK law, which is designed to capture the legal aspects of collaborative working and using an iterative, incremental development approach, is available on the DSDM website.

There must always be the ability to reach a compromise in what is to be delivered. If development is working to tight time constraints and new requirements surface, the solution providers (whether internal or external) cannot simply add them to the existing list of things to do. If they are really important, then agreement as to what can be dropped from the existing list has to be achieved. A collaborative approach is needed to ensure that what is essential will be delivered.

2.1 KEY POINTS

- ◆ The nine principles are a cohesive set and should all be applied on a DSDM project.

- ◆ The nine principles are:

   1. Active user involvement is imperative.

   2. DSDM teams must be empowered to make decisions.

   3. The focus is on frequent delivery of products.

4. Fitness for business purpose is the essential criterion for acceptance of deliverables.

5. Iterative and incremental development is necessary to converge on an accurate business solution.

6. All changes during development are reversible.

7. Requirements are baselined at a high level.

8. Testing is integrated throughout the lifecycle.

9. A collaborative and co-operative approach between all stakeholders is essential.

Chapter 3

The Process in Action

3.1 WHEN TO USE DSDM

DSDM is not the panacea to all project ills that developers are often promised. There are classes of system to which the framework is most easily applied and these are the areas which an organization which is less experienced in agile development should focus on to begin with – unless of course the pressure to deliver is so great that an 'unsuitable' project must be tackled before the organization is mature in its use of an agile approach, and DSDM in particular. The framework has been used on a wide variety of projects in a diverse set of organizations. It is difficult to say that the framework should never be used for a particular sort of application or platform. Whenever this sort of statement is made, someone always turns up shortly afterwards and says, 'We did it!' Indeed the Consortium has a motto: 'You can use all of DSDM some of the time and some of DSDM all of the time.'

The framework is more easily applied to business systems than to engineering or scientific applications. However, where the organization has a good track record in building such systems, it is not impossible to apply DSDM – just a little harder because of some of the criteria involved in filtering out unsuitable systems. The online manual contains a Suitability/Risk List that contains questions to ask when considering the use of DSDM on a particular project. The questions are under three headings: business, systems, and technical. The detail of the Suitability/Risk List is not discussed here, but the main questions to ask when deciding on the appropriateness of a proposed system to DSDM development are:

1. Is the functionality going to be reasonably visible at the user interface?
   Of course the user interface includes reports as well as screens or indeed any other way of showing the end-user what is happening inside the system. If users are to be involved throughout the development process, they must be able to

verify that the software is performing the right actions through prototyping, without having to understand the technicalities of what is happening behind the user interface.

One project that was suggested by a large manufacturer for their DSDM pilot did not demonstrate this characteristic. The organization had a comprehensive system for collecting quotations from component suppliers. The system allowed buyers to enter the details of what they needed in terms of engineering specification, quantities to be provided, frequency of delivery, etc. Requests for quotes from selected suppliers were then produced by choosing 'Print'. The buyers would then stuff the paper specifications in envelopes and send them out. The organization had decided that this process could be improved by the use of electronic messages. The only change to the process as far as a buyer was concerned would be that the final step would be a 'Send' operation, which would deliver the specifications to the suppliers electronically rather than through the mail. This operation would not be able to be verified by a buyer through inspection of the user interface. It would have been possible to capture the message for verification, but this would have gained very little benefit from the buyer's point of view. They only need to be assured that the messages are received at their ultimate destinations.

Two examples follow of projects with hidden functionality that could be run using DSDM because the approach was well embedded into the IT departments and they were able to think more laterally about how to achieve the correct level of user involvement.

The first project was rebuilding the back-end infrastructure to a ticketing system with no changes to any of the user interface. This seemed at first sight to make DSDM impossible. However, the users on this project were particularly adept at reading system activity logs and these would supply them with sufficient information to assess what was going on.

The second project was building some supplementary functionality to a batch, mainframe system (using CICS, DB2, and C). This involved a long series of extracts, loads, and sorts. The business people on this project were excellent users of SQL and were therefore able to 'watch' the data change and movements. This project was interesting from another point of view as it already had an agreed functional specification before deciding to use DSDM. If it had built what was stated in the functional specification, the wrong solution would have been delivered – and it would have lasted three more months (if nothing had slipped) using the same development team. The business people on this project never want to see a waterfall project ever again.

So for experienced users of DSDM, this question really means 'How can you make the functionality visible?'

2. **Can you clearly identify all classes of end-users?**
   It is essential to involve users within the project who can represent all of the potential end-user population. This has caused some concern when developing systems for widely disparate or geographically dispersed populations. However, with care, this is not insurmountable, as will be discussed in Chapter 7. The important thing is to ensure that you can obtain complete coverage of all relevant user views within the development team. Otherwise there is a danger of driving the development in a skewed direction. Moreover, the review process of sending out documents for a matter of weeks to a wide user group is very often not feasible on a DSDM project. Such reviews will seriously limit the chances of delivering on time.

3. **Is the application computationally complex?**
   This is possibly one of the hardest questions to answer. What is complex for one organization is simple for another. A lot will depend on what is available in terms of building blocks to the development team. The important thing is not to develop too much complex functionality from scratch. This question is closely linked to the first question about the visibility of functionality. For instance, if the system is performing complex actuarial calculations, this could render the project difficult for DSDM. On the other hand, if the calculation processes have been used in previous systems and are tried and tested, the actuaries will trust what is presented to them.

   For example, someone who was working on a large insurance project attended a DSDM Regional Investment Group (RIG) and stated that the insurance calculation parts couldn't be done using DSDM. Immediately someone chipped in who was working on a project for another insurance company with the comment 'The users in our team are underwriters and the developers are ex-underwriters, so we are doing *everything* using DSDM.' As we said at the beginning of this chapter, as soon as you say you can't do something using DSDM, someone will be able to prove you wrong. This time it was rather quicker than usual, if you replace actuaries with underwriters!

4. **Is the application potentially large? If it is, can it be split into smaller functional components?**
   DSDM has been used and is being used to produce very large systems, but in every case it has been possible to develop the functionality in fairly discrete chunks. There are several DSDM projects in progress at the time of writing that have a development period of two to three years. This could be viewed as not being *rapid* development, but increments will be delivered at regular intervals rather than waiting until everything is complete before the system is put into operation. The focus is on delivering what is most important first and what will deliver the greatest business benefit now.

If the system is large and there is no possibility of incremental delivery, i.e. everything has to be delivered in a matter of months for the system to be useful, then it must be possible to break down the work for development by parallel teams. Indeed, in large systems, there are likely to be parts that have to be developed using waterfall methods and this will force a degree of parallel development on the project. The introduction of parallel working has significant impact on the level of control that will be needed.

5. **Is the project *really* time-constrained?**
It is all too easy for business management to say that a system must be delivered by a certain date when they don't really mean it. This is potentially disastrous for the project. It means that while the developers are geared up to follow the DSDM guidance, the end-user participation at all levels is not as forthcoming as it should be. At best this is frustrating. At worst, the project goes in the wrong direction because the drive from users is not there and developers start making assumptions about what is needed in order to keep active.

With users in the development team, they can see the effort that the developers are putting in. Hence, they have a greater understanding of what is possible within the timescale. The result is that they are more willing to compromise on what will be in the delivered system. Without time constraints, they will not see any reason for compromise and will demand that everything be done. This will cause delay and inevitably the business benefits to be gained by the new system will be postponed.

6. **Are the requirements flexible and only specified at a high level?**
This could be reworded as 'Do you have complete understanding of everything that must be delivered?' Whatever the project, the answer is just about always 'No!' but, for DSDM to work successfully, the level of detailed understanding at the outset of the project should be lower than is the norm. This question was left out of Version 1 of DSDM and many experienced agile developers felt that they had been cheated by the framework. This has now been put right, but we need to look at why this was considered so important.

The use of prototyping with knowledgeable users to elicit requirements as you go is fundamental to the approach. If everything is understood and all the detailed requirements have been agreed and fixed before the software builders come on the scene, major benefits of DSDM will not be achieved, such as building the right system rather than what was originally requested.

Also, if the requirements are inflexible, it will not be easy to negotiate what can be left out if the project deadline is approaching and a great deal of work remains to be done.

3.2 *THE REALITY OF ITERATION AND INCREMENTAL DELIVERY*

As stated earlier, iteration is a fact of life in all IT projects. It is just that going round the same piece of work to attend to an earlier error in understanding is guarded against in traditional approaches to development. However, just because it is a fact of life, that doesn't mean to say that it is an easy thing to control. Many developers like the freedom that accepting iteration provides, but without the necessary controls they can run away in the pursuit of perfection, which may not actually be realizable. One non-agile project from some years ago suffered from just this problem. It was decided that, with the move from green screens to a graphical user interface, they should use a more user-centered approach to development without thoroughly thinking through the completion criteria for their prototyping activities. The prototyping part of the project took on a life of its own and became unrelated to the other analysis and design work that was taking place in parallel. This caused enormous friction, as it became unclear which part of the development team had the lead at any one time.

With all prototyping activity, you must decide on the evaluation criteria that are to be used when demonstrating a prototype or putting it into the hands of the users to investigate. This has been accepted practice within the human computer interaction (true HCI!) community, but has not always filtered out to the 'mainstream' developers. Fortunately, with DSDM, the timebox provides a defined scope of work, a mandated stopping point for iteration and defined completion and acceptance criteria. The use of timeboxes is discussed in more detail in Chapter 4.

DSDM has clearly addressed how to control iteration through timeboxing. It does not address the issues involved in incremental delivery. This is because incremental delivery has no distinct DSDM flavor other than the fact that not everything may be delivered in an increment. However, a few words here about the subject may be worthwhile.

Incremental delivery is extremely valuable in delivering quality working systems to the business faster. Nevertheless, it does increase the load on what the development team has to do. Instead of working steadily towards a single goal, there are repeated points when a complete and consistent set of documentation, working software, user manuals, training materials, etc., must be available. The effort involved in this should not be underestimated but, with the tool support available today, this is not the problem that it used to be.

3.3 *ANALYSIS AND DESIGN TECHNIQUES*

One of the things that has contributed to the wide acceptance of DSDM is the fact that it does not mandate a particular set of techniques to be used in an Agile project. Rather it takes the view that agility is about using what you know and understand well, but managing the day-to-day activities of analysis, design, building, and testing differently.

Hence, if we consider just analysis and design techniques for which there is a multiplicity of variations in both structured analysis and design methods and object-oriented methods, any of them can be adapted and used within the framework of DSDM. The important aspect that DSDM puts forward is to decide what constitutes the minimum set of analysis and design models necessary for the safe progression towards delivery and the minimum set required for maintenance purposes.

The minimum set for these are defined as the core models. These will be reviewed and checked as they grow incrementally towards the final system. Many other models are used simply to sort out the ideas of the developers and therefore do not need to undergo rigorous checks to ensure that they are right. These are defined as support models. If a developer has drawn a support model in her workbook just to clarify what is happening, the time taken in fully documenting it and reviewing it will be a bar to rapid movement towards the goal of delivery. This means that careful thought has to be given at the start of the project as to the documentation needs of the project and maintenance.

If we consider the core models for maintenance first, the question to ask is 'What do maintenance staff need to see to carry out their job successfully?' The first answer is a resounding cry from all maintenance staff that they trust very little beyond the code itself. So the code must be readable and well documented so that they can see what it is supposed to do. To support the code, other useful documentation typically covers an overview of what the system does, a context diagram to show its interfaces with other systems, a description of what the components of the system are, and the links between those components, the physical data structures, and the design decisions that were taken and why. Anything else is likely to gather dust on the shelves. Your project may be different so this list is not prescriptive in any way. Indeed, much will depend on the characteristics of the system itself and the toolset used to develop it.

Quite often, the design decisions are viewed as unnecessary for maintenance purposes, but there are projects that can provide a strong argument for including them. For example, in one case the database designers decided not to use indexing. There was a very good reason for this, which it would be too complicated to explain without taking a couple of pages to explain the system. Unfortunately, every time someone new came to look at the system, one of the first questions was along the lines of 'Wouldn't indexing be useful?' The loop would be gone round again and again. The design decision was recorded, but it was in a short paragraph in a very large document. Maintenance staff rarely read through large documents, which have become irrelevant over time; they only want to see the code. So maintenance core models should be kept lightweight, but complete enough to help new maintenance staff to understand the system as quickly as possible.

The same is true for the core models for development. Given the set of core models to be produced for maintenance, the project needs to consider what additional models need to be produced for development to move forward with a common understanding both within the team and between the team and interested external parties.

Certain models are fundamental to the process of development. For instance, in a structured analysis method working towards a new database, the data model is crucial, but many of the detailed process models can be swiftly overtaken by events. In a small system, a high-level data flow model together with a context diagram (defined above as a maintenance core model) will often be enough to support the team in understanding the external interfaces, the partitioning of processes and the sharing of data. Because analysis models and functional prototypes are being produced in parallel, as long as the code is well constructed and well documented, the detail of processes can be in the code. Again, the set of core models will depend on the characteristics of the system and the toolset used to produce it.

In an object-oriented approach, it is difficult to imagine a system without the classes defined in the core model set, but other diagrams such as event traces can be regarded as support models unless there is a particularly complex or fundamental event that needs to be documented. The set selected will again depend on the application and the development tools.

The selection of core models should never be driven by the pre-existing culture. In other words, just because a particular model has always been produced by previous software development projects, it does not mean that it must also always be produced in DSDM projects. What must be decided is which documents are essential. The set of core models can be very small in DSDM because many of the documents that are produced before the introduction of the framework are there to pass ideas from one class of team to another. Analysts produce detailed analysis models to pass their ideas on to the users for agreement and to designers as the basis for their work. Designers produce design documents to ensure that programmers do exactly what is necessary. Programmers produce detailed program specifications so that the designers can agree that they are doing the right thing and so that testers know what needs to be tested. And so on. And so on.

A DSDM team is a fixed team containing users and developers who have between them all the major analysis, design, programming, and testing skills required. As a result, the need for documents to pass ideas around is lessened. An additional benefit is that the common complaint from analysts that their work has been ignored and the counter complaint from programmers that the analysis work was a waste of time and had to be discarded are both non-existent in a DSDM project. The important different views from different roles are available throughout development.

3.4 KEY POINTS

- ◆ DSDM is particularly suited to business applications which demonstrate the following characteristics:

  1. are interactive, with the functionality visible at the user interface;

  2. have a clearly defined user group;

  3. are not computationally complex;

  4. if large, possess the capability of being split into smaller functional components;

  5. are time-constrained;

  6. have requirements which are not too detailed or fixed.

- ◆ Iteration is controlled within DSDM through timeboxing and does not run away in an uncontrolled manner.

- ◆ Incremental delivery can deliver business benefit early, but it introduces additional work on deliverables.

- ◆ DSDM does not mandate any set of development techniques.

- ◆ Core models provide the minimum set of documentation necessary for safe progress through development and for ease of maintenance.

- ◆ The core models and support models for development and maintenance need to be agreed before development begins.

- ◆ Core models need to be reviewed for content and accuracy; support models do not.

Chapter 4

Time Versus Functionality

4.1 FITTING QUARTS INTO PINT POTS

Keeping within time limits does not mean working faster or for longer hours than would normally be the case. Yes, the pressures will be there to work very hard and indeed, as the project progresses, the chances are that developers will occasionally work very long hours to meet their deadlines, but this can happen on any project, whatever the method being used. Long working hours should not be taken as the norm for DSDM developers. The aim should be to work within the normal working day and to keep weekends and evenings free. To do this you need to change the way that work is managed at all levels: the project, the team, and the individual.

At the project level, the focus is on ensuring that the scope does not expand beyond what is achievable. It is essential to get the scope clearly agreed during the business study. This is the basis for all decisions about what is possible in the time available. It often happens that during the later phases as the users get a better understanding of what the system will do for them, that they ask for more things to be added in. When this happens, it is not the project manager's job to reach for the change control procedures and to enter into negotiations for more staff or more time. The time has been fixed for whatever reason, and bringing in more staff will endanger the delivery on the agreed date. Frederick Brooks stated this in *The Mythical Man-Month* published in 1975, and still it is thought to be a solution! He pointed out that, if you bring new staff on to a project, time will be spent bringing them up to speed with the rest of the team. This must be done at the cost of the work that the original team members were planned to do.

So we don't ask for more staff and we don't ask for more time. The only thing that can happen is that, if the new request is really necessary, something gets left out of the work that was originally envisaged. We certainly don't want to let quality suffer, so the work that is left out is delivering some of the originally agreed functionality. Section 4.2 shows how to do this using the MoSCoW rules.

At the team level, the priorities of the functional and non-functional requirements are used to decide what the team should be doing at any one time. As an empowered group of people, they can decide on what work needs to be done and by whom. The team members work together to satisfy the highest priority requirements. Having regular and frequent team meetings is essential to ensure that the development is on track. Daily meetings of up to half an hour may initially be seen as an unnecessary overhead on the 'useful' work, but many issues can be resolved very quickly in them and they help the staff think of themselves as a team rather than a set of individuals. The daily meetings are really a formalization of the chat by the coffee machine, where it is well known that good ideas and expert knowledge can be gathered from other people. If the team opts for weekly meetings, a week's work from one person may be found to be in conflict with something that somebody else is doing and will have to be revisited. It is no good thinking that people will automatically talk to each other just because they are in the same team.

One worst case example of uncommunicative (and therefore uncollaborative) teams involved a non-agile project where a team of four analysts were working at a group of four desks with no partitions between them. So they were facing each other all day, but they didn't talk! Three of them were doing the process analysis and one was assigned to data analysis. They had been working for three months and the project was experiencing considerable slippage. None of the process analysts had discussed the interfaces of their process areas with the others, and the data analyst was working completely separately from the rest of the team. Not surprisingly, they had all gone over much the same ground and had wasted considerable effort in resolving issues that were common to them all. Even weekly meetings would have helped this unfortunate group who were carrying out personal tasks set by the project manager rather than working as a team.

At the individual level, the developers and the users have to accept that it's not possible to do everything. Developers who want to investigate every single detail of an issue and focus on the automated system because that is what they understand and who cannot move to only doing what is absolutely necessary to the business will find DSDM a very stressful way of working. Not only that, they will also disrupt the activities of other team members who are more user-focused and who accept that doing enough is the winning strategy. Unfortunately, there is no way of knowing whether a developer will take to DSDM until it has been tried. Some people take to the ideas immediately. Others take a month or so. One DSDM project was severely handicapped by keeping on a developer who had an excellent track record in programming and was very quick to learn new technical skills, but who just could not handle the fact that he had occasionally to limit his view of what was necessary. Worse still, he viewed the users changing their minds about something as a major irritation, which stopped him doing what he was there to do – design, build, and test programs. The attributes of agile developers are discussed in Chapter 10.

4.2 TIMEBOXES

There are several current definitions of timeboxes. One that is prevalent is the time between the start and end date of the project. The end-date is inviolable and a system will be delivered on that date. DSDM has taken the concept of timeboxes further by nesting them within the project's overall timebox to provide a series of fixed deadlines by which something will be delivered, where the 'something' could be an analysis model (partial or otherwise), a part of the front end, a completed area of functionality, a combination of these, or indeed anything that moves the project nearer its target of delivering a useful system on a given date.

In DSDM, timeboxes are typically between two and six weeks in length: the shorter the better. However, the limits are not inviolable. One over-zealous project auditor raised an objection to a timebox that was planned to be seven weeks long. This did not matter as long as the project manager and his team agreed that that was the minimum time required to do the work. The major advantage of keeping timeboxes short is that it is easier to imagine what can be done in the time.

It takes nine months to have a baby. While they are waiting for the baby to be born, parents will spend a considerable amount of time choosing clothing, a cot, a mobile to hang over the cot, cuddly toys, etc. If, however, parents were told that they could expect a baby in one week, they would focus attention on what they could purchase during the week and be sure of having the essentials ready for the new arrival. It is this style of thinking that makes timeboxing an effective way of carrying out successful projects in short timescales. For some reason, it is far easier to envisage what you can do in a short period of time than to be given a task and then decide how long it will take you to do it. Hence, the timebox is a useful tool in the process of estimating the resources needed to achieve the operational system.

An important aspect of timeboxes is that they are not activity-based. The aim of a timebox is to make something. How that thing is put together will be decided by the people doing the work. This is one way that the third DSDM principle about focusing on frequent delivery of products is applied.

4.3 MoSCoW RULES

MoSCoW is an acronym for the prioritization that the requirements are assigned. The 'o's in MoSCoW are just there for fun. The rest of the word stands for:

- ◆ **'Must have'** for requirements that are fundamental to the system. Without them the system will be unworkable and useless. The 'must haves' define what DSDM calls the minimum usable subset.

♦ 'Should have' for important requirements that would probably be classed as mandatory in less time-constrained development, but the system will be useful and usable without them.

♦ 'Could have' for requirements that can more easily be left out of the increment under development.

♦ 'Want to have but will not have this time round' for those valuable requirements that can wait till later development takes place.

All of these requirements are needed for the full system. The 'wish list' does not appear in the categorization. The important thing about the MoSCoW rules is that they provide the whole basis on which decisions are made about what the developers will do over the whole project and during any timebox within the project.

To give a practical example of applying the MoSCoW rules, we could consider building a domestic video cassette recorder. The 'must haves' (i.e. the minimum usable subset) would be recording television programs, rewinding tapes, and playing them. The VCR just will not operate without these capabilities. The 'should have' would be the facility to record while away from home. This definitely enhances the value to the user, but the VCR will be usable without it. The 'could haves' would be facilities such as fast forwarding and pausing. They add to the ease of use, but are not essential. The 'want to haves' would be a remote control, automatic tracking, etc., all of which could be added later.

4.4 CONTROLLING TIMEBOX ACTIVITY

Given the above, timeboxes are really requirements satisfaction boxes in which something will be achieved. Each timebox passes through three phases. The three phases are:

♦ **Investigate** where a quick first-pass is made to check that the activities inside the timebox are going in the right direction.

♦ **Refine** in which the results of the investigation are improved and as much of the deliverable is produced as is possible in the time.

♦ **Consolidate** which is the final part of the timebox. Here the aim is to make the deliverable complete and consistent within itself and, if it is part of the time-box's objectives, to check that it fits with other deliverables.

The functional model iteration and the design and build iteration phases pass through several cycles of: identify what you are going to do; agree how to do it; do it

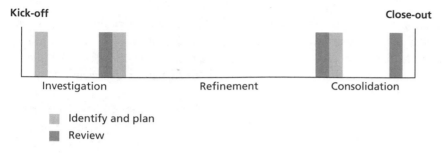

Figure 4.1 *Timebox schematic*

and check that you did it (and obviously you should be able to show that you have checked that you did it). This cycle appears in each of the three phases within a timebox. So, each timebox phase starts with an objectives-setting meeting (Identify and plan in Figure 4.1) with all members of the team who are participating in the timebox, and finishes with a review of progress and products.

The kick-off meeting for the start of the timebox is the most critical for objective setting. It is at this point that the team considers what the timebox was originally planned to produce. At a minimum, this meeting is for the timebox team (Team Leader, Developers, Testers, and Ambassador Users). Most kick-off meetings will also be attended by the project manager and the Technical Co-ordinator. Key timebox kick-off meetings will also require the presence of other key individuals such as the Visionary.

The first task of this meeting is to review what has been achieved in any previous timebox which delivered related products and to check for any impact on the work of the current timebox. Some of the dependencies may cause the deliverables from the current timebox to be rethought. For instance, it may be that previous work has identified the need for a new mandatory component or, conversely, that a part of the planned deliverable in the current timebox does not have the necessary prerequisites available to allow it to be delivered.

Having checked the deliverables for the timebox, the relative priorities of the parts of the timebox deliverable are re-assessed to see whether or not they are still valid and their relative priorities are checked and possibly re-assigned using the MoSCoW rules.

Another key decision made in this initial objectives-setting meeting is what the various quality criteria are that the deliverable must demonstrate to be acceptable at the end of the timebox. The agreed quality criteria are prioritized using the MoSCoW rules. In the case of a timebox delivering a software component, the quality criteria in effect define the test cases that will be applied but the detail of the test cases is left for later. This cannot be done at this time since it is not known exactly what functionality the software component will finally contain – particularly true of the 'should haves' and 'could haves'. A new 'must have' could arise during the time-box and displace some 'must have' which is seen to have a lower priority in reality.

The schedule for the timebox is confirmed on the basis of this more detailed under-standing of the timebox's objectives and deliverables. In particular, the review dates are set. Having done all this, everyone at the kick-off meeting has to agree that at least the minimum can be delivered. If not, then a quick decision has to be made about what should be done. This could involve replanning and reprioritization of remaining work.

It is very important that not all things to be done in the timebox are 'must haves'. If they are, the content of the timebox should be revisited. The team must feel confident that if things do not go entirely to plan, there is something that can be left out while they focus on sorting out the essential components of the timebox deliverable.

The last part of this important objectives-setting session is to agree what the investigation phase will deliver. This could be as informal as a set of models on a whiteboard that have been developed collaboratively by the Developers and Ambassador Users. At the other end of the spectrum, it could be a highly formal speci-fication together with a full definition of the tests to be run by the Ambassador Users.

At the end of the investigation phase, the checkpoint assesses the initial deliver-able and notes any necessary changes to the timebox deliverable or its acceptance criteria that may arise. Back to back with this checkpoint, the objectives are set for the refinement phase. It is in this phase that the real meat of the timebox deliverable is tackled. The product is built, tested, documented, and reviewed within the team.

At the end of the refinement phase, the review again assesses progress and deter-mines what actions are necessary to achieve completion according to the acceptance criteria. It is very useful to consider the review at the end of the refinement phase as the end of the timebox. This gives some leeway for inevitable slippage – particularly for those things many developers put at the bottom of the list, such as documentation.

The final phase of consolidation starts with an objectives-setting meeting, which decides what must be done in the remaining time to ensure that the deliver-able will meet the minimum acceptable quality criteria. No new work should be started during consolidation: this phase is 'just' for tidying up loose ends. The checkpoint at the end of consolidation is used by the timebox team to validate what they have done and will present to the close-out meeting.

The close-out meeting is attended by all interested parties, in particular those people who are empowered to accept and sign off the product of the timebox. The accept-ance is dependent on the satisfaction of the quality criteria set at the kick-off meeting.

How timeboxes are controlled from the project management point of view varies from one organization to another. Two examples of timebox control documentation that have been used are included here. One was used by the Department of Health in its pilot DSDM project (Table 4.1). This project had done some extensive analysis before the decision to move to DSDM was made, so this form very much concentrates on controlling the design and build aspects of the system which produced statistics about usage of certain parts of the services of local health authorities. The rest of this section shows a timebox control sheet used by an investment bank during a large project to create a new equities settlement system. The example is partially completed to show how they were used.

None of these forms is considered the definitive answer to all timebox controls. Interestingly, the project manager on the UK Department of Health project worked for Xansa which is one of the largest third-party software maintenance suppliers in the UK and she included the maintainability target. So the message is 'control what is important to you'.

Timebox Specification (Department of Health)

Function to be prototyped:	Ref. in Functional Spec:
Start date: End date:	Tech. effort allowed:
Dependencies:	
OBJECTIVES: (1) (2) ...	
Outcome:	
Priorities: (1) (2) ...	
Outcome:	
CRITERIA: (1) (2) (3) ...	
Outcome:	

Table continued on next page

Timebox Specification Continued

Agreed minimum useable subset: (x-ref to Objectives)	
PERFORMANCE TARGET: **(1)** **(2) ...**	
Outcome:	
MAINTAINABILITY TARGET:	
Outcome:	
QUALITY REVIEW METHOD	User sign-off after 3rd iteration; Technical review of code by:
1st iteration: (date) **2nd iteration: (date)** **3rd iteration: (date)**	(record initials of those present)
Documentation updated: **RQ (date)** **FS (date)**	
DELIVERABLE produced: **FILED in:**	(file name/version no.) (library)

Timebox Specification (Investment Bank)

Control sheet for timebox nn.

Version History

Version	Date	Author	Status	Description
0.01		Timebox Team		First version for review.

Version History Continued

0.02		Timebox Team		Second version for review, Business requirements & technical specifications *(used iteratively)*
0.03		Timebox Team		Third version for review & technical specifications
0.04		Team Leader		Final version

Sign-off History

Version	**Date**	**Signature**	**Name**	**Role**
0.01	09 March 2001			Visionary
0.01	09 March 2001			Ambassador User
0.01	09 March 2001			Team Leader
0.01	09 March 2001			System Architect
0.01	09 March 2001			Technical Co-ordinator
0.01	09 March 2001			Project Manager

Purpose of this Document

This document will be marked as 'final' when the final timebox deadline is reached and will be used as the formal sign-off document at the close-down meeting in conjunction with the completed test-summary document and a list of the relevant items from the current MoSCoW list. It contains a list of all the deliverables (MoSCoW items) that have to be addressed in this timebox with a summary for each of what comprises the deliverable and the criteria to be met to prove that the MoSCoW item is satisfied. Where items were not delivered, then the reason is noted here.

It also holds:

♦ The critical dates as agreed at the timebox kick-off meeting and a brief description of what is to happen on those dates.

♦ Links to the business requirements and main technical design documentation produced during the timebox.

This timebox lifecycle document will be used as a control sheet for the referred timebox as well as a reference point for future use.

Timebox Exit Criteria (Full Details in the Testing Strategy Document)

Item	Actioned by	Signed by
Test summary document	Team leader	See sign-off above
Timebox control document	Team Leader	See sign-off above
Outstanding issues list	Team Leader	N/A
User reviews	Team Leader	See review minutes
Test case/script delivery	Users – see 'Acknowledgements'	See test summary
Ambassador user testing	Ambassador User	See test summary
Advisor user testing	Advisor User	See test summary
Merge/regression test	Team/Tech Co-ordination	See test summary
Close-out meeting	Team Leader	See minutes
Technical documentation	Team members	Tech Co-ordination
User documentation	Users	Tech Co-ordination

Acknowledgements

A list of people involved in discussions or e-mail correspondence with the Timebox Team during the production of this document.

Status of the Timebox Documents

(Comment status indicating the current state of the documentation between 'does not exist' and 'final/signed-off')

Status of the Timebox Documents

Item	Status
Business requirements:	In progress
Technical specifications:	In progress
Test data gathering:	In progress
Test scripts/programs:	In progress
Final documentation (this document & test summary):	In progress
User documentation:	In progress

Timebox Schedule

Description	Start date	Completion date
Timebox nn kick-off meeting		
Requirements gathering		
Complete test summary sheet		
First draft of timebox control signoff document and circulate		
Review meeting 1		
Test case delivery		
Review meeting 2		
Final review		
Stop timebox nn development		
UAT and regression testing on team image by Ambassador User		

Table continued on next page

Timebox Schedule Continued

UAT and regression testing on team image by Advisor Users		
Final sign-off		
Close out meeting for timebox nn and kick-off meeting for timebox nn+1		

Deliverables/Acceptance Criteria

The deliverables for this timebox are as per the MoSCoW list. Further details are held in the Timebox nn Working Document.doc, which also includes a list of milestones for the timebox, and a breakdown of the high-level MoSCoW items into a detailed MoSCoW list for this timebox.

Items Carried Forward – Non-MoSCoW Items

A live list of outstanding timebox team issues can be located in a timebox team issues list. There are no scheduled issues for this timebox. Rather, issues will be tackled as time allows.

Timebox MoSCoW items

The box below is repeated for each requirement within the timebox.

Timebox of MoSCow Items

Timebox	Requirement no.	Requirement	Priority	Status
Identifier from development plan	From prioritized requirements list	Simple title for requirement	M/S/C	Started/in progress/ tested/reviewed/accepted
More detailed description of requirement. Built during timebox, under constant review.				
Acceptance criteria: Prioritized during the kick-off meeting and changed/confirmed at investigation phase review.				

4.5 TO TIMEBOX OR NOT?

Some activities which are essential to the success of a project are just not possible using the timebox approach. It is not acceptable, for instance, to have only part of the interface between the client and the server working. One of DSDM's early adopters' projects was the development by Sysdeco of a newspaper production tracking system by Sysdeco (UK) for the Boston Globe. The system was developed from scratch in four months using DSDM, after an attempt by another organization to tailor an existing system had failed after 18 months. DSDM was used for the user-facing components of the system, but it was also necessary to build a data daemon which would transfer status information from existing systems through standard interfaces. The data daemon that would perform this function had to be 100 per cent complete or be useless. Moreover, there was no simple way of involving users in the validation of its functionality. Therefore, it was developed in parallel using more traditional development methods. DSDM should not be used to the exclusion of all other methods and definitely not where it is inappropriate.

4.6 THE DISASTER SCENARIO

The crunch question that is always asked about timeboxes is 'What happens when a major new "must have" surfaces during development and there is no slack left in the other requirements?' The questioner almost always seems to expect the answer that time will have to slip to accommodate the new requirements. Fortunately this is not the answer. What happens in practice is that a swift renegotiation of the priorities is undertaken with all interested and influential parties involved. In the majority of instances the new 'must have' turns out not to be a showstopper as far as the timescales are concerned. If the system really does need it, then something will be done to fit it in. This usually means that something else has to go. In the rare projects where timescales have had to slip, the management may decide that the time slippage is more acceptable than delivery of a system without the added requirements. This is possible when the business need for the earlier date has disappeared. Wherever time is of the essence, something is left for delivery a few weeks or days later. The first increment will perform the short-term solution for later modification.

4.7 KEY POINTS

- ◆ Short timeboxes within the overall project timebox are the means of controlling the quality of interim products and avoiding scope creep during development.

- ◆ Keeping timeboxes short facilitates effort estimation.

- Timeboxes have a cycle of investigation, refinement, and consolidation.

- All requirements are prioritized to ensure that the most essential requirements are satisfied first.

- Quality criteria are assigned to each requirement, and prioritized independently.

- The deliverables from a timebox are tested and/or reviewed within the timebox, rather than afterwards.

- Activity within timeboxes should be defined in terms of deliverables rather than tasks.

- Some development activities cannot be managed easily using the timebox approach.

Chapter 5

People Working Together

5.1 A POTENTIAL FOR GLOBAL CHANGE

A DSDM team consists of developers and users working together, but this is not the whole picture. DSDM prescribes a 'no-blame' culture and defines a philosophy for collaborative working that reaches far beyond the parochial concerns of an individual project team. When adopted whole-heartedly, it can change a whole corporate culture to become a more communicative, effective, and open working environment, overcoming the artificial barriers that exist in many organizations.

5.2 THE PROJECT ROLES

DSDM defines several roles, some of which are for development staff and some for the users. A team is kept small in order to shorten the communication lines between team members. Typically a DSDM team consists of two to six people. The minimum is two because there must be one person to do the technical work and one user to ensure that the work will satisfy the business needs. The maximum is six because this is what has been found to be the limit beyond which the process has difficulties. A project may, of course, have more than one team.

No distinction is made between the different IT roles: analysts, designers, programmers, etc. They are all categorized as Developers. The other development role within the team is that of Tester, who provides independent testing of technical aspects: the functionality is tested by the users. Developers will naturally test their own work in the early stages, but before it is passed to the Ambassador Users for their testing, it will have been through an independent testing within the development area.

A key IT role is that of Technical Co-ordinator. This role defines the system architecture, is responsible for ensuring that the project is technically consistent and that all work produced is of sufficient technical quality. In particular all Testers report to the Technical Co-ordinator with results of testing activities within their teams. The Techincal Co-ordinator is also responsible for ensuring that technical controls, such as configuration management, are used effectively.

Being a user-centered approach to development, DSDM has defined several user roles to work both as part-time advisors and to participate within the project team. The key user role within the team is the Ambassador User. Ambassador Users are so named because they operate in very much the same way as diplomatic ambassadors. They have the responsibility of bringing the knowledge of the user community into the team and disseminating information from the team to the rest of the users. They are not the sort of full-time staff used in some organizations as an information channel between the developers and the users. An Ambassador User comes from the community that will use the delivered system. Identifying the correct people to fulfill this role is fundamental to the success of any DSDM project.

DSDM defines another key user role, that of the Visionary. The Visionary is probably the person who initiated the project through their vision for new ways of working in their business area. The Visionary may not be the purse-holder and ultimate decision-maker in the business area – that is the role of Executive Sponsor. The Visionary participates early on in the project (during the feasibility and business studies) to ensure that the right decisions are made as to what is important and what is not. Later, the Visionary participates in key demonstrations and meetings to ensure that the team does not lose sight of the original business objectives.

Users have traditionally sat outside the development team providing their knowledge during requirements gathering, reviewing work in progress, and performing acceptance testing. The number of users who can be involved in these activities can be quite large in order to cover all necessary user views. DSDM recognizes that the holders of the Ambassador User role may not cover all necessary viewpoints, so an additional role of Advisor User is defined to cover the disparate views that may exist. Advisor Users are anyone who has an interest in the final system. This could include IT staff such as system administrators and support staff, or 'fringe' business staff such as financial auditors. Advisor Users will be involved on an ad-hoc basis as required by the needs of the project.

The detail of all these roles together with their responsibilities and required skills are contained in the DSDM online manual. A skill common to all roles is that of effective communication. Developers of all types must be able to listen effectively and communicate their ideas in non-technical language. Users must be competent at expressing their own needs and the vision of the business.

5.3 PROJECT STRUCTURES

A typical DSDM project will have one or two teams, but a large project can grow to as many as six teams, all working in parallel. Again, like the maximum team size, six seems to be the limit beyond which things start to get unmanageable. However,

DSDM has been used effectively on projects of a much larger size, with the addition of the more formal communication channels that this increase in scale necessitated. One such development had more than 150 people, both business and IT, working to build a new line of business.

Where there is only one team, the Technical Co-ordinator role will be within the team and is likely to be carried out by the most senior technical expert. Where there are two or three teams, the Technical Co-ordinator role may still be filled by just one person, but that person will be outside the teams, working in a managerial and technical advisory capacity. When the project has more teams, the role of Technical Co-ordinator will probably be split between different specialist staff. One possible way of splitting the role on a large project would be to have three people taking up different parts of the role: one would be the system architect; one would be responsible for assuring the technical quality of what is produced; and the other for controlling the developing software and document configuration.

With multiple teams it is often useful to have one team doing co-ordination work. For instance, one team could take the role of database administrator. Some DSDM projects have opted to have a separate testing team. This is difficult to make work successfully in 'vanilla DSDM', since every software deliverable from a timebox should have been tested within the timebox to demonstrate whatever objectives had been set for the timebox. The objectives could demand elements of system testing, integration testing, and regression testing – not just unit testing. There are obvious disadvantages to working this way. Most importantly, if testing uncovers an area requiring rework, to what timebox can the rework be assigned? There just shouldn't be the slack in the plan to allow this sort of activity to be accommodated – unless, of course, the timeboxing approach is diluted. By all means a large project can have a team of 'flying testers' who are pulled into timebox teams to see that tests are adequately carried out, but this should not be done after it has been agreed that a deliverable meets the quality criteria set at the beginning of the timebox.

Each team should have the technical and business skills necessary to perform the core of what they need to do. There may be a need for additional specialists to be called in as required. For instance, having a reuse broker could be very useful if the organization has its reuse strategy well organized. Another useful external expert could be a human computer interaction specialist to ensure that the user interface is designed for maximum productivity, ease of use, etc., as well as looking at the wider issues concerning the operational environment. The support from specialists will depend on the nature of the project and the skills of the core teams.

If the project is using a development tool for the first time, it is advisable to have technical support for the team arranged before they start work. It is often the case that DSDM projects introduce new technology alongside the new process. Some such projects have had near disasters through not being able to make the tool behave in the way that they thought it should and through having poor support from the tool suppliers. However, do let the developers learn.

One project very sensibly trained all the developers in the new tool that they were going to use and brought in an expert to support them as they enhanced their knowledge throughout the project. Unfortunately, his productivity was ten times greater than that of anyone else, so they let him do major parts of the development. Consequently he had limited time available to solve the problems that arose among the novices. This was not a strategy to make future projects in that organization work more effectively with the new tool.

It is extremely valuable to have an external facilitator for running facilitated workshops (see Chapter 7). When the person running a facilitated workshop has an invested interest in the way that the project is going, it can be very difficult for the workshop to gain the consensus that is needed. Sometimes project managers may go into facilitated workshops with a list of objectives, which include 'Get the users to agree to X'. This is against the whole ethos of DSDM. It could be that X is not what is needed. An impartial facilitator will uncover more easily that Y is the solution and will gain agreement to it. The arguments put against using facilitators who are external to the project is that they cannot know all the details of the project. This is true. However, the very best example of a facilitator at work we have seen was getting a room full of about 60 people agree to a way forward on a topic about which the facilitator had absolutely no knowledge at all – in under two hours. Achieving consensus from 60 people in such a short time is dramatic enough. The fact that the discussion was completely outside the facilitator's sphere of knowledge should convince the sceptics that having a trained facilitator is more important than using someone with detailed project knowledge.

5.4 KEY POINTS

- ◆ DSDM defines roles and responsibilities for both users and developers.

- ◆ Key roles which are DSDM-specific include:

    1. The Visionary (a senior user) to ensure the overall business objectives are adhered to.

    2. The Ambassador User to bring business knowledge into the team on a day-to-day basis throughout the project and to communicate to business colleagues.

    3. The Technical Co-ordinator to ensure that all work fits into the system architecture and meets the required technical standard.

- ◆ DSDM teams should be no more than six people, including the Ambassador User(s).

Chapter 6

The Agile Project Manager in Action

6.1 WHAT IS DIFFERENT?

Since time is fixed and resources are mostly fixed, the project manager's job is somewhat different from that in a traditional project with a more relaxed timescale. All the skills that make a good project manager are still required, but the focus is slightly different. Moreover, with an empowered team, the more autocratic project manager has no place heading up a DSDM project. The responsibilities of the project manager are the same: careful planning, close monitoring of progress, keeping the team working effectively, awareness of the risks to be managed, etc. What is different is the way that planning is carried out, how progress is monitored, the style of management for an empowered team, and what the specific risks are in a project.

The DSDM project manager has a significant logistical challenge. There are a multitude of shorter tasks involving more parties than usual over a very confined time frame. It is the responsibility of the project manager to ensure that all the right facilities are in place at the right time for the team to work effectively. For instance, the time between the start of analysis and the building and testing of software is very short – the facilities for these different activities must be in place when they are needed. There is very little room for logistical delays in a project.

One area where project managers traditionally spend a lot of effort is on trying to prevent drift from specifications that have been signed off. This leads to strongly enforced change control procedures. DSDM is all about enabling change to occur without the confrontation that has often arisen through adherence to a specification. Project managers who are new to DSDM worry a great deal about how to stop the scope expanding beyond what is achievable in the overall timescale of the project. The previous chapter on timeboxing should have laid many of the concerns about controlling the scope to rest. All we can do is assure the novice DSDMer that it does work and has been proven on many projects.

6.2 *PLANNING A DSDM PROJECT*

DSDM defines four points in the process where project-planning activities are undertaken.

1. In the pre-project phase, the activities of the feasibility study (and possibly the business study) are planned.

2. As part of a check on the feasibility of the project, an outline plan is produced to provide confidence that the project has the likelihood of success.

3. During the business study more information is available about what has to be done and what the relative priorities of the work components are. The Development Plan is produced.

4. Towards the end of functional model iteration, it is clear what will actually be delivered in the increment. The Implementation Plan is produced to cover all activities necessary to move the project's deliverables from the development environment into operational use.

Before leaving the business study, the outline plan produced during the feasibility phase is refined to take account of the additional information. The Development Plan includes the schedule of timeboxes and the working practices to be used, such as testing and configuration management strategies. The detailed planning of timeboxes is the responsibility of the relevant timebox team and is carried out 'just in time' since it is very difficult to say well in advance what the detailed activities will be within a given timebox. Also, the dependencies between timeboxes may make it impossible to carry out some planned work because the preceding requirements have been left out of a timebox.

The functionality to be delivered will have been identified by the end of the business study. Clear prioritization must be achieved during the business study.

All functionality should be placed into functional groupings, which should be kept as small as possible. Each grouping should have its components clearly prioritized so that it is possible to leave lower-priority parts out of the grouping if all does not go to plan. None of this prioritization can be done by the project manager, either alone or with the developers, in isolation, as the business imperatives are what drive this decision-making process. Indeed leaving it to the IT staff can lead to a technology-driven approach which will not facilitate working with the users to deliver the system.

Design considerations may occasionally override business considerations as to what is most important. Some functionality will necessarily appear in more than one functional grouping. For instance, a simple enquiry as to the status of a particular item may appear in several business processes. Functionality that appears regularly in several areas is probably fundamental to the success of the system and assumes a high priority, however trivial it may seem to the overall business processes.

Other functions that are obviously given a high priority are those which are seen as critical to the success of the increment. However, this criticality should never be taken at face value. The questions to ask are 'Is there a possible workaround if this functionality is not available?' and 'Does this have little or no material impact on the business case for the project?' If the answer is 'yes' to both questions the functionality is assigned as low a priority as possible. The aim of prioritization, is to ensure that the 'must haves' are as small a set as possible with the other levels of optionality well understood.

The prioritized functionality also provides the basis for deciding what architectural components must be present in the delivered system. For instance, if it is essential that some information from another system is available then the interface to that system must be possible. The architectural components should ideally be available before the functionality that needs them is built. Therefore, the prioritization of the functionality will drive the prioritization of the system architecture components. However, there will be some components which are acknowledged to be important, but which cannot be aligned to particular system operations. Some non-functional requirements (such as performance) may well have architectural impacts that cannot be assigned to one area of functionality. When these are to be addressed, and their relative priorities, will depend on when they can be easily fitted in with other work.

The architectural requirements should be as clearly prioritized as the functionality. There should always be the possibility of moving away from a previously agreed technical approach if things prove difficult. For instance, in a modeling project for an oil company, the developers were having real problems with getting the modeling tool that they were using to provide the right statistics. It was, in fact, buggy. So given that the timebox was nearing its end-date, the developers swiftly moved to providing the information through a spreadsheet for manipulation by the users: a less sophisticated solution, but one which was acceptable in the short term. It was acceptable also within the architecture since the chosen spreadsheet was part of the standard platform for the end-users.

Some non-functional requirements may apply across all work, such as usability or maintainability. It is useful to assign these requirements to every timebox since they will keep the developers focused on the overall quality objectives of the project.

There are several schools of thought about what to do first. One is that tackling something easy first gives the developers a boost and encourages further work. The problem with this approach is that it leaves the difficult areas until later and providing solutions to these may invalidate some of the earlier work. Another approach is to identify the major technical risks in the increment and to tackle these first. This has the advantage that if something needs to be rethought, then there is time to do it. However, it can mean that key business issues are not addressed early enough. A third approach is to produce something that is fundamental to the business requirements. This will provide the users with early visibility of the developing system and will enable them to verify that the right direction is being taken. For systems with little technical risk, this is the best approach. Where the technical risks are high, a combination of the second two approaches should be used, spreading the technical risks across the first few timeboxes while developing as much visible functionality as possible within that constraint.

As with any project plan, the project manager should identify what human resources are to be used. The users should be assigned to the areas of functionality that fit their business knowledge. Given their advisory role, they can be assigned to more than one concurrent timebox. Developers should never be assigned to more than one timebox at a time. Furthermore, if developers are from a general resource pool and have other calls on their time, the successful delivery of the products of a timebox is unlikely. The project manager should strive for dedicated technical staff wherever possible. The tight timescales of a timebox make external activities a significant risk to completion.

Having decided on the order in which parts will be delivered and who has the relevant skills (technical and business), the next task is to allocate the work to a set of timeboxes. A crude first pass is achieved by simply dividing up the development time into timeslots of, say, two weeks. Each timeslot is potentially N timeboxes where N is the number of parallel timeboxes that are possible with the resources available. Each timeslot should have allocated to it a mix of mandatory and less essential work that makes a sensible group of related products. How each group is chosen is totally dependent on the application under development and the architectural and business dependencies that have been identified earlier. Nevertheless, a mixture of 'must haves', 'should haves', and 'could haves' is essential to the timebox approach. If everything to be produced in a timebox is a 'must have', there is no room for maneuver if things do not go well in the timebox. Of course, all the usual project planning constraints need to be considered, such as holidays and the availability of hardware and software. If it is possible that users will be unavailable for participation in a particular timebox, there must be a decision escalation route in place. How this will work will depend on the culture and organization of the business.

Having allocated work to the initial timeslots, the next step is to test the feasibility of the plan with the developers who will carry out the work. The question to ask here is whether or not an arbitrarily chosen number of days is sufficient for the work to be achieved. The key is not to allow them to lengthen the timeslots by building in contingency. The contingency is already contained in the fact that not everything is necessarily delivered. If the developers want a timeslot lengthened, they should be able to justify the extra time. It is common for the first timeslot to be longer because of necessary groundwork to get the work under way. However, this should not be necessary if a known environment is being used, a 'standard' system architecture is being applied, and the business functionality is not too complex.

Where the duration is accepted as sufficient, the developers should be asked if they can reduce it and still be reasonably sure of delivering the work. If the project manager is as technically expert as the development team, it may be possible to refine the durations without reference to the developers. However, this can lead to the developers feeling that unrealistic timescales have been imposed on them. It is possible that the plan now extends beyond the end-date for the project, in which case, the resourcing levels need to be rethought, the scope of the project needs to be revisited, or the relative priorities of deliverables need to be reconsidered. The business needs will be paramount in this process.

The detail of when the deliverables from timeboxes will be reviewed, tested, and accepted is left until the timebox is initiated. However, overall procedures for these activities need to be in place. If these are either not standard to the organization or not already agreed for the project, they should be documented now and associated through document management procedures to the timebox plan.

In addition to who will carry out the day-to-day work within a timebox, the people who will be responsible for monitoring and control of the activity must be nominated, as must the people who will have the authority to accept work from the timeboxes.

A normal project planning tool can be used to show some components of the plan: resources, parallel working in timeboxes, and timescales. This should be supported by documentation to show the optionality of work within the timebox. This can be a simple table showing for each timebox 'must haves', 'should haves', and 'could haves'. Alternatively, timebox control sheets, such as those shown in Chapter 4, can be produced in skeleton form now.

6.3 MANAGING RISK

Most procurers of IT systems are concerned with two risks. These are that the system will not meet the needs of the business and that the project will overrun on time and/or cost. Correct use of DSDM counteracts both of these risks. Systems that meet the needs of the business are delivered through the incremental and iterative approach with its continuous feedback from users. Cost and time overruns are avoided by the use of timeboxes.

This does not mean that managing a DSDM project is a risk-free activity. In the main the risks arise from not complying with one or more of the underlying principles of DSDM followed by a failure to implement risk mitigation activities to allow for the non-compliance. The online manual includes strategies for mitigating these risks as well as other more general risks. One highly experienced DSDM practitioner claims that this is the most useful part of the online manual.

The first port of call for risk identification is the DSDM Suitability/Risk List. This will enable the project manager to keep a vigilant eye on the factors discussed in the section on 'When to use DSDM' and other potential areas of concern. It is first examined before the project starts and is revisited formally at the end of both the feasibility and business studies. The end of the business study includes a major 'go/no go' review of the project in which if the level of risk is deemed unacceptable, the project should be terminated. The Prioritized Requirements List provides another tool in risk identification that will help the project manager to focus on the risks associated with requirements that have a high prioritization. The output of all risk identification, categorization, and assessment activities throughout the project is recorded, as in all best project management practices, in the Risk Log, which is opened in parallel with the first review of the Suitability/Risk List. For projects considered to be 'small', it may be deemed that the Suitability/Risk List without the generation of the Risk Log provides sufficient means for recording and monitoring the risk. It may be prudent to categorize the risks for the risk identification process. The categorization would be dependent upon the size of the project. For instance, for small projects the categorization may be limited to business, systems, and technical. These risk categories could then be respectively owned by the Visionary, the Ambassador User, and the Technical Co-ordinator.

6.4 MONITORING PROGRESS

Once the project manager who is new to DSDM understands how to plan the activities of the project and what the team should look like, the next major area of concern is how to make sure that everything is working out. The key point to remember is that time is not the issue here. There is little point in asking a team member 'How much longer is this going to take?' because the answer is supplied by the end of the timebox in which he or she is working. What needs to be monitored is how much of the minimum usable subset is being achieved, i.e. how many of the 'must haves' have been satisfied at any one time.

The main tool for deciding on progress is the prioritized requirements rather than a Gantt chart of activities. The Gantt chart will show the timeboxes and the personnel associated with each timebox, but the supplementary documentation about what is to be produced in each timebox is far more important for control and monitoring purposes and is product-based rather than activity-based.

For high-level project information, the prime method of monitoring and reporting progress against the requirements is through the satisfactory completion of timeboxes. If timeboxes are given clear objectives and methods of demonstrating achievement of those objectives, there is nothing better than the end of timebox documentation to show that progress is being made. This is also easily understood by high-level management as evidence of progress. Additionally, the users in the team provide an informal channel to their own management and the wider user population for progress reporting and monitoring. The Ambassador Users will be fully aware of the progress being made both as they sign off the deliverables from timeboxes and as they participate in the ongoing activities within the timeboxes.

For more detailed, working-level monitoring and control, the best mechanism has been found to be a daily meeting of the whole team. This should be short and sharp and held either at the beginning or at the end of the working day. Typically these meetings last 15 minutes – sometimes they can be as short as five minutes but never more than half an hour unless a major issue needs to be discussed. The meetings are more effective than the project manager asking each individual how work is progressing since areas of common concern can be identified by other team members. There can be times when the team members feel that these meetings are a waste of time and that they should be getting on with the job, but project managers should stick to their guns and hold the meetings regardless.

The DSDM pilot section at British Airways had a very useful rule to be applied at their daily meetings. Nobody was allowed to say, 'I am doing this task at the moment.' They had to say 'I have done this task' – however small. The rule has two advantages. First, the project manager is getting real evidence of progress. Second, nobody likes to come to a meeting where they are the only person unable to report success. The result of the second point is that each team member is continually striving to have something achieved. This keeps the momentum of the project going. If someone turns up at the meeting with nothing to report, then there is probably an issue for the project manager to address.

6.5 WORKLOAD

A frequent concern of project managers who are new to DSDM is that they will have to ask the team to regularly work overtime. If the project has been properly estimated and risk avoidance strategies put in place, this should not be the norm. There are no doubt organizations where the culture is to arrive as late as possible in the morning or to leave as early as possible in the evening. This will not work in a

DSDM environment unless all involved are keeping the same hours and achieving a full working day. The day can be far more concentrated than many staff are used to and as with all time-critical activity, there will be occasions when you have to call on the team to work longer than usual. However, as one project manager said to a DSDM consultant, 'You warned me against burn-out and said that the team should be given something more restful to do after a DSDM project. What you didn't say is that they wouldn't go back to more traditional working.' Longer hours do not mean more productive work is achieved. However, many developers enjoy DSDM projects so much that they will want to work longer hours – to satisfy their professional pride as much as anything else.

It is not only the developers who will be working in a more concentrated way. If the organization is used to having project managers manage several projects at once, the scope of their responsibility will have to be drastically reduced. Even a very small DSDM project can be a full-time job for the project manager. Every day there are more things that need the project manager's attention because of the speed with which products are delivered. Any problem that arises must be dealt with immediately. Another project manager said that he would normally be able to manage five projects of a similar size to his current DSDM project, which kept him busy a hundred per cent of the time.

6.6 KEY POINTS

- ◆ Project planning is based around the timebox.

- ◆ Functional and non-functional requirements should be grouped and allocated to timeboxes.

- ◆ The 'contingency' in timeboxes is contained in the lower priority requirements that may not be satisfied.

- ◆ Estimating the length of timeboxes should involve the team.

- ◆ Risks associated with cost and schedule overrun are avoided by the DSDM principles and process.

- ◆ A key resource for risk management is the DSDM Suitability/Risk List.

- ◆ Progress should be monitored daily.

- ◆ The concentration of work for all concerned is often greater than on traditional projects.

Chapter 7

Impact on the Organization

7.1 MAKING DECISIONS

The major impact on many organizations that implement DSDM is in the way that decisions are made about the direction that a project takes. Such decisions are made throughout the life of a project and they have to be made very quickly indeed, if the project is not to falter. For the decision-making processes to operate speedily, DSDM's second principle of empowerment of the team should be rigorously applied.

If the culture of the IT solution provider is to allow only major decisions to be made by a project board (or a similar body), then DSDM will significantly increase the demands on the project board's time. DSDM projects that have worked within such an environment have found that one or two members of the board have had to be contacted for decisions several times a week. This is obviously not ideal as, at best, it affects the working day of important people within the organization or, at worst, delays decisions because those people have other tasks to carry out for the good of the organization.

If the culture does demand the use of project boards, the board members should have their responsibilities clearly defined. This is normal practice, but the 'standard' responsibilities should be assessed for their validity in DSDM. It is a common complaint of board members of early DSDM projects in an organization that if the team is empowered, then they do not have any authority. Involving them effectively is as necessary as involving the Ambassador Users in the team. So what does a project board do in a DSDM project? Board members have responsibility for finance and are called in if significant changes to the original plan are envisaged. The Ambassador Users are making decisions on a daily basis. They are accepting work as it is produced rather than a few weeks later at a formal project board meeting. Only the team should make decisions at the day-to-day level and the project board should be confident that such decisions do not affect detrimentally the cost of the project, nor the proposed business benefits. Frequent reports from the project manager will build that confidence. The frequency of reports will depend on the speed with which the project is operating, but they will probably be produced every one or two weeks. A simple one-page status report should suffice.

A strongly hierarchical organization, where people work within well-defined grades or ranks, can make it very difficult for the 'lower orders' to take responsibility for the decisions that they are required to make during a project. In this sort of organization, the Ambassador User will probably not come from high enough up the organization to have been allowed to make decisions in the past. Such an Ambassador User can feel very unsure of where the limits of their responsibility lie. It can initially be very frightening for someone of this kind to feel that their decisions must be accepted by those higher up in the organization. Often, they are right to feel unsure. Terms of reference must be given to the users operating within a hierarchical organization. These should clearly state where the limits of decision-making lie.

In several instances, empowerment has been given lip service only. The team are assured by all relevant senior staff that their decisions will be accepted, but when it comes to the crunch, this is not the case. Some senior managers are very reluctant to delegate responsibility to their staff. For some reason or other, this appears to be particularly true of IT management. They are more than happy for the business members of the team to be empowered, but are firmly against empowering their own staff. The only way that delegation by senior staff can be improved is through education. Such education could be by running a one-day DSDM awareness course, but really senior staff may not feel able to attend. Another route is to have a DSDM expert spend an hour or two explaining to senior members of staff the advantages to be gained from loosening the reins a little.

How decision-making at the team level is made to work will depend on the organization concerned. Just a few pointers are provided here. The basic requirement is to trust the people who have been assigned to perform a particular role and for others to be sure that the trust is well founded. As stated in the ninth principle, collaboration and co-operation between all stakeholders are essential.

7.2 USER INVOLVEMENT

The second major impact on the organization results from releasing staff from their usual work to supply the necessary time to the project. The level of involvement should be as high as possible, without seriously affecting the work of the business area in which the users normally reside.

The problem is that the users who will participate as Ambassador Users will usually be key staff within their area. If it is easy to get the time from an individual, then that person is probably not the one the project needs. This is a real 'Catch 22' situation. DSDM advocates full-time involvement in the project but, in the lean organizations of today, this is very often impossible. The important thing is to get a continual flow of information and feedback from the user community throughout the project.

The right people for the project are those individuals whose decisions will be respected by the rest of the user population and who have sufficient business knowledge to see 'the wider picture' wherever possible. Someone who is to represent a user community should be able to do just that. They should not be focused on the minutiae of their own work to the detriment of other users' needs. If we were to produce a work-flow system for a tele-marketing department, the ideal Ambassador User is a supervisor. A tele-salesperson may be too focused on the way the job is done now. The supervisor's manager is probably too divorced from the detail of what has to be done by the sales staff. On the other hand, the supervisor will have good knowledge of their daily work and should have a broader view of the department's operation than they do. The Ambassador User will discuss the project regularly with the other end-users so their points of view will be captured, but it is important that the day-to-day decisions are made by someone with the correct breadth and depth of knowledge.

The supervisor is essential to the running of the department, but she is also essential to the project. A compromise has to be reached. Given that a project will not be of long duration (unless it faces years of incremental development), it is possible to get key business staff into the team, but usually though some sort of 'contract' for their time. Some real project examples follow.

One project had identified a very senior engineer as the Ambassador User. He was already working very long hours and could not afford to give up any of his day to the project. He made a contract with the development to arrive at work an hour earlier than his and their normal start time. Another project was building a system for traders. Traders cannot afford to lose any of their working day because time really is money in their business. So the Ambassador Users on that project spent time with the developers after business had closed for the day. Yet another project was building a system for a part of the UK civil service that had faced stringent cutbacks in staff. There was absolutely no fat in the organization at all. The solution for one of the Ambassador Users was to make time available 09:00 to 10:30 on Monday, Wednesday, and Friday. If the development team did not request his presence by 09:10, the time would be used for the Ambassador User's normal work.

The problems of getting a sufficient level of involvement from the right users are compounded when there is a very large user population. This is made even worse when a new system will affect a population that spans all levels of an organization. Very careful classification of all the users' needs to be made to ensure that all relevant views will be available to the project. It may mean that to have total representation requires having a group of Ambassador Users who significantly outnumber the developers. This will not work. In addition to assigning the minimum number possible of Ambassador Users to participate in development, the project should set up a User Panel who have frequent visibility of what is going on inside the development. One project which covered several regional centers within a very large organization had a user panel which met the Ambassador Users every Friday, at a location which all could reach within three hours.

When the system is for implementation across national boundaries, then e-mail, video-conferencing, etc., are ways of involving the users, but they are not the only solution. There should still be someone in physical – rather than virtual – contact with the team. One example of building in the right level of user contact was devised by Sysdeco in its Early Adopter project. The developers were based in Cambridge, UK, but the customer was the *Boston Globe* in America, so they worked the other way round. The team put an 'Ambassador Developer' into the *Boston Globe*. He carried out the front-line analysis work with the users and, through the use of e-mail, he could demonstrate the latest work of the development team. While the software was being demonstrated, he would have 'control' of development and would be able to make changes that were then sent back to the UK.

Essentially, if it is not worth the users giving up time from their normal jobs, the user management should consider whether or not the project is really worth doing. If it is, then there is usually a way of getting DSDM to work in the way it should. Perhaps the Sysdeco example is one of the most imaginative.

7.3 BETTER COMMUNICATION

DSDM speeds up the development process, through shortening the communication lines between all parties involved. There are various ways in which this is achieved, but the prime objective is to make sure that the barriers that can stand between users and developers are just not present.

One major barrier that often exists is the barrier of language in the documents that are produced by IT for users to read and sign off. By bringing users into the team, so that they can visualize more easily what IT are doing for them, eliminates the need for many documents. It is far easier to question the meaning of something when the person is speaking to you than when a document arrives on your desk without sufficient explanation of some of the more jargon-ridden parts.

Another barrier is that large project teams must use formal, documented communications to be sure that everyone is aware of what is going on. The production of these documents can be time consuming and will therefore necessarily delay the transfer of information from the writer to the intended audience. By using small teams, a DSDM project can rely more heavily on informal communication that can be faster and more efficient in ensuring that everyone knows the current status of the project activities and of its deliverables.

An effective small team will usually be more creative, particularly if as many viewpoints as possible are contained within the team. DSDM ensures that the key IT roles are present throughout the project, rather than that the relevant business views are easily accessible. Collocating developers and users wherever possible shortens the communication lines between the business and IT. It is far easier to ask a question of somebody if they are nearby than when they are at the end of a phone line. One rather young and shy developer needed to have a question answered by the Visionary, which had held up development for three days. He had sent several e-mails and left various voice-mail messages with no response. He asked for advice on this communication breakdown and the solution was simple. The Visionary worked in the next building, so it was necessary to simply walk across and wait for a break in her work to ask her the question, which was answered immediately. The problem was solved, taking about 15 minutes in total.

7.4 FACILITATED WORKSHOPS

Bringing people together who have the right knowledge to avoid misunderstandings is the foundation of the whole approach. A very useful method of bringing such people together is through facilitated workshops. Gary Rush, in his paper on JAD workshops (1985), said that workshops for capturing requirements can take about one fifth of the elapsed time of traditional techniques. Without having any metrics to support it, this is probably a conservative estimate of the saving in elapsed time. Perhaps this is because of the more sophisticated technology that is now widely available to speed up the production of documents arising during workshops.

There is a great deal of literature and advice available on how to run facilitated workshops and the topic is also covered in the DSDM online manual, so it will not be dealt with here in detail, except to talk about the use of facilitated workshops in DSDM. James Martin divides up the workshops into joint requirements planning (JRP) for capturing the business requirements and joint application design (JAD) for the later technical workshops. In DSDM, a facilitated workshop can be at any point in the development process, from project inception to delivery, wherever it would be useful.

The aims of a facilitated workshop are to produce something and to achieve consensus among the participants as to the content of that thing. It is particularly useful in the business study, when the foundations of the project are being built. If one area of the business is to have its requirements placed at a lower level than another's, facilitated workshops will enable that sort of decision to be made without rancor. The first place in DSDM where they are beneficial could be during the feasibility phase. This depends on the number of decision-makers that should be involved. Even before the project is under way, a strategy workshop to decide on a program of projects and what needs to be done by when can be very useful indeed.

During the business study, facilitated workshops are an excellent vehicle for obtaining an understanding of the processes to be supported and potentially automated, together with their information needs. How the processes are modeled will depend on the techniques that the organization finds most useful. One agile team in Norwich Union (a large UK financial services company) used pictorial views of the components of the system, which were readily understood by the business participants in a workshop. A letter would be a picture of a letter, a role would be a picture of a person, etc. These are similar to the rich pictures in Soft Systems Analysis. Other organizations use business object models, data flow diagrams, or swim-lane diagrams to show the flow of information and the transfer of authority between different business components. Use what you know and what you think the workshop participants will understand. Concerns about using technical modeling techniques are usually unfounded. If a model is being built up in front of the users, it is very easy to explain the syntax as you go along.

Workshops can achieve the seemingly impossible. In one case, a facilitated workshop was run for an organization that had a set of discrete systems, which it wanted to integrate for better information flow between the various departments. The workshop was attended by each of the department heads. A corporate data model was put together from scratch in about half a day. Admittedly it was in need of later refinement, but it gave sufficient information to understand most of the information needs of the organization.

Later on in the process, facilitated workshops can be used for prototyping the user interface. Again depending on the technology support you wish to use, this can be through the use of anything from whiteboards or Post-its on flipcharts to fully automated screens. There are tools available that have been specifically designed for the agile development of user interfaces. One example takes images from a magnetic whiteboard picture of the desired windows, buttons, etc. and generates the necessary code.

It is important to decide what the workshop is for and if it is valuable to take business participants away from their normal work. IBM use facilitated workshops for a multitude of activities both inside and outside DSDM, including business vision analysis, business process re-engineering, information systems strategy study, benefits analysis, requirements definition, technical systems options, acceptance test planning, service level agreements, and team-building. This is not an exhaustive list, but it should trigger ideas about when facilitated workshops can be used effectively. For the purposes of DSDM, it is worth picking out the combination of benefits analysis and requirements definition. It is often hard to decide on the priorities of the system. If benefits analysis has been carried out before the definition and prioritization of requirements, such decisions can be far easier to make and, in some instances, can make themselves. KnowledgePool has used facilitated workshops for other activities, such as determining the content and logistics of a training program for a very large user population, and change management to encourage new ways of working after installation of the new system.

7.5 TRAINING USERS

For user involvement to be successful, it is advisable that all parties who will be involved in the project are fully aware of their roles and responsibilities in DSDM. This can best be achieved by running a one-day DSDM awareness course. The value of setting aside a day for training at the start of the project cannot be underestimated. It brings to the surface many of the issues that might otherwise remain in doubt.

Two examples from DSDM projects can illustrate the need for training. In one project, the awareness day completely changed the attitude of a key user who had been 'bitten' by IT once too often. At the beginning of the day, he did not understand the level of influence that he would have throughout the project and was opposed to the idea of a new system. By the end of the day, he saw that he might get what he really needed this time. The system has now been delivered and he is a real champion of everything that it does. On another project, it was the user management who had their attitude changed. They had been told by the IT department that a branch supervisor would be needed to work with them for three days a week throughout the project. They had agreed to this, but it was not until the awareness course that they saw why it was necessary. Indeed one manager said at the end of the session, 'They really mean it!' The comment suggests that the user management would not have been wholehearted in their support of the DSDM approach. Without the awareness days, both of these projects would have probably not achieved the necessary user involvement, or at best the user involvement would have been only on sufferance.

7.6 KEY POINTS

- ◆ Decisions that are not in the control of the immediate project team must be made very quickly.

- ◆ The continuous involvement of Ambassador Users is essential to the success of DSDM.

- ◆ Ambassador Users must have sound business knowledge and should be respected by their colleagues at all levels.

- ◆ 'Contracts' for their time should be agreed at the outset and adhered to.

- ◆ DSDM shortens communication channels between all parties both inside and outside the team.

- ◆ Facilitated workshops are a powerful means of achieving this.

- ◆ It is advisable to train all the users who will be involved in the project so that they understand their roles and responsibilities.

Chapter 8

Never Mind the Quality?

8.1 'GOOD ENOUGH' SOFTWARE

The main aim of DSDM as a framework is to remove the 'quick and dirty' image of agile development. This is achieved through a strong focus on delivering what is needed, when it is needed, while ensuring an agreed level of maintainability is built into the software and its supporting documentation.

Traditionally, quality-related activities have striven to drive out all identified defects before delivery. Much of the work of quality assurance and control is aimed at ensuring as low a defect rate as possible. Such an aim may not be possible in the timescales of a DSDM project. That does not mean that developers are delivering unusable software that crashes every day, or that requires the users to save their work every few minutes in fear of loss of data at the desktop before it is sent to the database. What it means is that a certain level of imperfection is acceptable. Software has to be 'good enough' – and no more or less. Defining what is good enough is often difficult and requires an element of pragmatism. However, if the business agrees that the functionality in the minimum usable subset has been provided adequately and the IT staff are happy that they are not going to be called in regularly to fix the non-business aspects of the system, then the system can be accepted. To achieve acceptance of the delivered system, it may be necessary to disable a malfunctioning item and postpone its delivery to a later date. It is permissible to do this only if the component is not part of the minimum usable subset that must be delivered.

All of the above means that a different approach to quality-related activities may be needed by an organization that is introducing DSDM.

8.2 BUILDING IN QUALITY

One of the areas in which a definite line must be taken by the members of an agile team is the level of maintainability that the system will demonstrate. DSDM defines three possible levels of maintainability and the one to be achieved on the project must be agreed during the business study, as it will drive the quality control activities for the rest of the project. The three levels are:

♦ the system must be maintainable from its first delivery into the operational environment;

♦ initially, maintainability is not guaranteed, but will be addressed after delivery;

♦ the system is a short-term fix and therefore will not be maintainable and the developers reserve the right to remove the system from production once it has served its immediate purpose.

The first level is obviously the most time consuming in the initial development and will demand excellent quality controls during all stages of development. However, the chances are that it will provide savings over the life of the system. The second one will deliver the first increment of the system faster, but may be more costly in the long term, since doing the same work in two passes will incur more overheads in implementation, etc.

If the second option is chosen, two things should be borne in mind. First, that even though maintainability is not an immediate issue, the future rebuilding should be remembered at all times in order to make the rework less troublesome. Records should be kept of parts that have been skimped with respect to maintainability. Second, the project must be sure that future funding is guaranteed to be available. If not, the use of the second level of maintainability should be seriously reconsidered. The maintenance staff will not want to take over a system which will be difficult for them to understand – even though that is what is asked of them all the time!

The third level of maintainability is the hardest to achieve in practice, but, if the user management has signed up to this approach, the suppliers must be determined in their efforts to take the system out of the production environment. It is essential that the system is removed at the time agreed. There are too many systems in operation which were built quickly to solve a specific problem and which remain in place causing endless headaches to IT departments as they try to keep them running effectively.

8.3 TESTING

IT management often worry that testing will be squeezed out as agile projects race to deliver. One of the principles of DSDM is that testing happens throughout the lifecycle and is not something which happens at the end – after all the decisions have been made about the content of the software. Timeboxes are the mechanism through which testing is a continuous activity throughout the development process.

Within a timebox, testing is performed simultaneously at several levels, from unit testing through integration and system testing to acceptance testing – not forgetting regression testing, which is particularly vital in an iterative approach to development. Paul Herzlich, who wrote the testing chapter in the original manual, calls this a 'broadband' approach to testing.

Unit testing is very similar to that carried out by developers in traditional projects. Additionally, if a component can be seen or exercised by a user in the team, then it is. This brings one element of third-party testing into the timebox. It is dangerous to pass the testing to a third party who is outside the constraints of the timebox. They may not have the same focus on the relative priorities of the timebox in terms of deliverables, quality criteria and timescale. This is why the tester role is part of the timebox team.

Integration testing also happens within a timebox if its software deliverables need to be integrated with a software deliverable from a preceding timebox. In this way, integration testing happens incrementally throughout development. Indeed, as development in timeboxes progresses, the number of components to be integrated will move towards the number in the system to be delivered. Hence the integration testing will move away from technical concerns about interfaces to concerns about integrated functionality. As the number of components increases, and as the components mature towards their target functionality, integration testing shifts in focus from technical integration of low-level interfaces to testing of the combined functionality of the overall product. In other words, it moves towards system testing.

At no time should a software component be delivered by the team without undergoing unit and user testing at the very least.

The presence of users in the team puts an early emphasis on validation as opposed to verification, which is the traditional mode of testing in the early stages. In other words, early on in the project, the users are looking forward to the viability of the system in use, rather than the developers focusing entirely on whether or not their code fits with previously defined specifications. This brings down the cost of fixing the sort of errors that are often discovered during the traditional user acceptance test at the end of a project or, worse, when the system is in production.

A perennial problem in user acceptance testing is that users do not understand how to produce test scripts. As Ambassador Users see how developers handle the testing of technical aspects of the system, they become increasingly competent in user testing. This education is one of the responsibilities of the Tester role, who assists in the design of user tests, but at no point actually writes them. The Ambassador Users are therefore ideal staff for putting together formal acceptance tests to be used by the wider user population when they are needed.

The overall effect of this approach is that often more time is spent in testing than would be considered the norm. If the testing techniques used are appropriate and focused on finding errors, rather than proving that something works as specified, the result should be a system that can be trusted in the operational environment.

An overall strategy for testing should be defined before any software is produced. This should cover everything from unit testing to acceptance testing. It is not possible to delay the strategy until later, or the work of timeboxes may be invalidated, instead of building confidence in the system as it is developed.

On large projects or because of contractual constraints placed on external systems providers, it may be necessary to cater for testing activities that are not contained within a specific timebox. If the strategy of testing as much as possible as you go is adhered to, the time for these activities should be minimal. There really should be no rework encountered, so the elapsed time should be just for running the tests – the least of a tester's worries during activities like contractual acceptance testing. For instance, a DSDM project manager from a major database company was contractually obliged to have a full month of User Acceptance Testing at the end of the project. The project had run all possible tests successfully during development, so as she said, 'It was money for old rope.' If rework is required, then the organization should look at its testing strategy and try to improve things on the next project.

Now for a bit of motherhood and apple pie! Many developers learn testing informally and are often surprised when told of the various approaches to choosing test cases. It is advisable, if testing is to work effectively, that at the very least the Tester in a timebox team has undergone formal training in testing.

8.4 DSDM AND TickIT

The TickIT scheme in the UK provides rigorous certification and third-party auditing procedures around the ISO 9001 standard, together with the ISO 9000–3 notes for guidance for software development. No large software house in the UK can hope to stay in operation without TickIT certification. The introduction of DSDM and its increased usage has caused some concern to the TickIT auditing companies, since many see agile development as a 'licence to hack' – completely contrary to all that TickIT stands for. However, as one large software supplier after another espoused the use of DSDM, it became obvious that such organizations would not want to jeopardize their reputations for delivering quality software and that there was something of value in DSDM for quality-conscious organizations.

The result is that the British Standards Institute produced (with assistance from the DSDM Consortium) a specific guide for the application and assessment of DSDM in a TickIT environment. There is nothing in the guide, *Dynamic Systems Development Method and TickIT*, which differs from the DSDM manual, it simply extracts and documents the procedures and controls to which the customer and supplier should conform and that the third-party TickIT auditor of DSDM projects should expect to see in place. None of these are in contradiction of the contents of the international standards, but the document provides a useful abstraction and collation of the many aspects of quality management that are within the text of the DSDM manual.

8.5 NEW PROCEDURES FOR OLD

The standards in an organization that relate to the quality of products will remain unchanged, but the standards relating to how that quality is achieved will probably have to change. Many existing quality management systems are firmly based on the waterfall lifecycle. They assume that there will be a detailed statement of requirements and a functional specification against which all deliverables will be assessed. As a result, the quality control procedures are focused on achieving satisfactory compliance to these documents. In DSDM, some software may be delivered before the requirements are documented for the full system and the functional specification is a much smaller document that also grows incrementally with the software. In fact, the functional model, which replaces the functional specification, is ahead of the software, but in many instances, only by a matter of weeks, and cannot really be used as an instrument for change control.

Change control is one of the areas most likely to be affected by the introduction of DSDM. This brings with it the need to reconsider the standard contractual arrangements with external suppliers or the basis of agreement as to what will be delivered by internal suppliers. For external suppliers, it is preferable not to choose a fixed price approach, as it often requires a detailed specification before design and development work can proceed. A more flexible approach is needed. Fixed price can be used, but the basis for acceptance probably has to be changed. For instance, some external suppliers use the number of function points delivered as the basis for acceptance, rather than complying with a document, which is liable to change until very late in the project. There are several approaches in use, but all of them require some change to the way contractual agreement can be achieved. At the time of writing, there is a draft contract template available on the DSDM website which is designed for the more flexible approach needed when contracting out DSDM projects.

It is based on UK law, but company lawyers from other countries will also find it of value.

Another area where standard procedures may need to change is in the area of testing. The previous section discussed the move away from the V-model of testing, where testing activity is related to the development stages in the waterfall lifecycle (see Figure 8.1). If the testing procedures are based on this approach, then they will need to be reconsidered. DSDM does not allow for discrete stages of testing. This is largely because instead of one big V-model for the project, there is a multiplicity of little V-models applied throughout development as timeboxes (or groups of time-boxes) take a tranche of requirements through to coding.

Testing activities will be just as formal as usual, but they may not be as formally documented prior to testing taking place. There is very little point in producing a test specification if the component to be tested is not produced. This reason alone will mean that procedures for testing may have to change. It is perfectly acceptable to define early on what the test will demonstrate and to document what the test actually does at the time it is carried out. Capture and replay tools are particularly useful in lessening the burden of testing documentation. As always, a log of test successes and failures should be kept to demonstrate the progress towards completion of testing.

To ensure auditability of the process and products, internal auditors should be involved in any changes to the procedures and in initial quality and project planning activities until an organization has 'bedded down' in the application of DSDM.

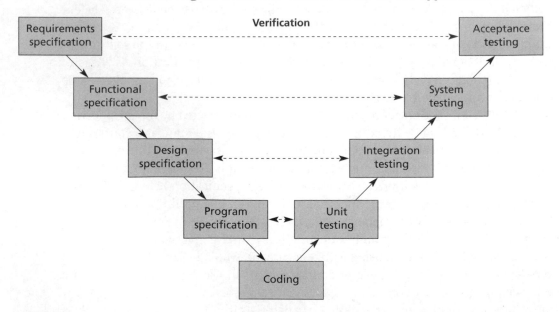

Figure 8.1 *The V-model showing which testing activities verify which specifications*

Where auditors who are external to the organization are involved, they too should be consulted if at all possible. They are stakeholders in the process and should be treated as Advisor Users.

8.6 *THE CAPABILITY MATURITY MODEL*

The Capability Maturity Model (CMM) developed by the Software Engineering Institute (SEI) at Carnegie Mellon University in the USA is the most common model for software process maturity. It encompasses the process management and quality principles into five levels, where every level has a number of key practices associated with it. Following is the main characterization of the CMM process maturity levels and the impact of adopting DSDM for organizations at these different levels of maturity.

1. **The initial level**, where the software process is characterized as ad hoc, and occasionally chaotic. Few processes are defined, and success depends on individual effort.

2. **The repeatable level**, where basic management processes are established to track cost, schedule, and functionality. The necessary process discipline is in place to repeat earlier successes on projects with similar applications.

3. **The defined level**, where the software process is characterized as standard and consistent. At this level, the software process for both management and engineering activities is documented, standardized, and integrated into an organization-wide software process. All projects use a documented and approved version of the organization's process for developing and maintaining software.

4. **The managed level**, where the software process is characterized as predictable. At this level, detailed measures of the software process and product quality are collected. Both the software process and the products are quantitatively understood and controlled using detailed measures.

5. **The optimizing level**, where the software process is characterized as continuously improving. At this level, continuous process improvement is enabled by quantitative feedback from the process and from testing innovative ideas and technologies.

Most organizations are at level 1 of the CMM. The DSDM Consortium believes that introducing DSDM into an organization can help the organization achieve process maturity level 2. Successful adoption of DSDM will inject a degree of process discipline in the organization and progress the process maturity of the organization to CMM level 2 or above. This is the level where a disciplined process is in place. (It is also the level where ISO 9001 operates at its most basic level of process maturity.) Once DSDM is established as a practice, the organization can aspire to improving its software processes to achieve higher levels of maturity. DSDM will help establish the main key process areas required for establishing a disciplined process. The mapping between level 2 of the CMM and DSDM covers all the key process areas specified by the CMM for level 2 as follows:

◆ requirements management, which is achieved through the Ambassador User role in the DSDM team;

◆ software project planning;

◆ software project tracking and oversight;

◆ software configuration management, which is a key feature of DSDM;

◆ software quality assurance;

◆ subcontract management, which is mentioned briefly in this chapter, but covered in more depth in the DSDM online manual.

8.7 KEY POINTS

◆ The focus is on building software that is sufficiently robust to be usable – and no more than that.

◆ DSDM builds quality controls into the process.

◆ Maintainability objectives should be agreed during the business study.

◆ Testing is earlier in the lifecycle than traditionally and incorporates all classes of testing from very early on.

◆ Introducing DSDM into an organization will probably mean that quality control and assurance procedures will have to change.

◆ DSDM fits well with both ISO 9000–3 and the CMM.

Chapter 9

Prototyping is not a Waste of Time

9.1 BRIDGING THE LANGUAGE BARRIERS

DSDM is more than anything about improving communications between all parties involved in the development of a system. Prototyping is one of the ways that communication between the developers and the users is made more effective. Because of the technical nature of their work, IT personnel use a language that is adapted for their particular needs, as in any specialist discipline. To the layman, this language is obscure. Moreover, the users often have their own language that relates to the business area in which they work. The users' jargon is often less arcane than that of IT, but communicating across this language barrier has been a perennial problem.

The use of diagrammatic analysis and design techniques has gone some way towards alleviating the problem. Indeed the use of diagrammatic techniques has evolved on the basis that a picture is worth a thousand words and a picture with syntactic rules is even better. Unfortunately, an interpreter is often needed for users to understand what the pictures mean and the accompanying text is often a hindrance rather than a help. The basic problem is that static abstractions of the proposed system do not easily convey the dynamic nature of the system under construction. A dynamic, working model of the system or part of the system is far more effective in showing the thoughts of the developers than a document or set of documents. We could say that a working model is worth a thousand pictures.

A further problem is the limited attention paid to the user interface by many analysis and design methods. The increase in interactive methods of working over the last decade has made the design of the user interface one of the deciding factors as to whether or not a system will be considered of operational benefit. The user interface is seen by the end-users as the way the system operates – whatever is happening underneath. It must match the way that users think and the way that their business functions.

While the layout and navigation around the user interface are obviously important, even something as simple as using the wrong word can create problems. For instance, in a system being put together for air traffic controllers, the developers used a 'Clear' button for clearing the screen. The air traffic controllers took this to mean that they were clearing the aircraft to land! Fortunately, the error was discovered during early prototyping. This is a powerful example of the misconceptions that different languages can introduce.

9.2 BUT THE USERS KEEP CHANGING THEIR MINDS!

The title of this section is a common complaint among IT staff. What is really happening is that as a part of the system is demonstrated to them, the users become more aware of what is being developed and what the system can do for them. It is very difficult to explain in the abstract what is needed. Could you describe a new machine that you have never seen before without the technical knowledge of the components necessary for that machine to operate successfully?

Managed effectively, timeboxing will ensure that the changes that are asked for are necessary and relevant to the task in hand. Minor aspects such as the color of objects at the user interface are immaterial and can be addressed later if they are seen to be important by the larger user population. Also when considering the minutiae of presentation, it should be borne in mind that the Ambassador Users are not always right. They are there to make sure that the system operates correctly and is easy for the users to operate. One user became so keen on the use of color (having previously been using green screens), that she demanded red and green to demonstrate the different statuses of the information. This could have been disastrous for color-blind staff. However, a change to the grouping and flow of information to fit the way that user community thinks about it, or a request for different information to be displayed, is not evidence of change just for change's sake. It is the Ambassador User realizing that things could be done better.

To ensure that the system is evolving in the right direction, it is a good idea to bring in different user views as often as possible. The Ambassador User provides the front line during prototyping, but when there is a key area being addressed, a demonstration should be given to the relevant Advisor Users. They may well ask for something to change, but it is better to find out early that a particular need has not been successfully addressed, rather than later on when it will be more difficult to incorporate.

The kick-off meeting at the start of a timebox should decide whether a wider user view is needed or not. The fact that timescales are tight or that the developers feel the prototype may not be elegant enough for a wider audience should not be reasons for deciding against a demonstration to the Advisor Users. If the knowledge of the Ambassador Users needs to be supplemented, then it should be.

9.3 CATEGORIES OF PROTOTYPES

DSDM uses the word 'prototyping' because that is the industry 'standard', but they are not truly prototypes: they are partial system components. A DSDM prototype is not 'all done by mirrors', but is built using the platform on which all the development work is done, and meeting all the required standards. In other words, the prototypes are intended to be evolutionary rather than throwaway: they will evolve into the delivered system. Of course, there will be occasions when it is better to throw something away and start again, but the aim at all times should be to build on what is there already.

Four categories of prototype are recommended by DSDM that are used at different stages of development, and have very different purposes. They are:

* **business** prototypes for demonstrating the business functions being built into the system;

* **usability** prototypes for investigating aspects of the user interface which do not affect the functionality;

* **performance and capacity** prototypes for ensuring that the system will be able to handle the workloads successfully;

* capability/design prototypes for trying out a particular design approach.

While the purpose of each prototype category is different, it will often be the case that some combination of them will be used. For instance, a common combination is the business and usability prototype, but this approach should not be taken as a matter of course. If the functionality is at all complex, it may be better to get it right before worrying about the presentation aspects. Conversely, if there is no standard for user interface design, it is a good idea to get some usability prototyping done first. The categories of prototype to be built in a timebox should be decided at its outset based on the aims of the timebox.

Because of their purpose of demonstrating functions, business prototypes are obviously produced during the functional modeling iteration.

The usability prototypes can be produced during both functional modeling and design and build but their primary usage will be during functional modeling – to gain user buy-in as much as anything. Also, leaving usability issues until later in the lifecycle can adversely affect the overall design strategy.

Performance and capacity are clearly design-based prototypes and belong in the design and build iteration.

Capability/design prototypes are in the category that is most likely to be thrown away. They can be produced at any time. They are used to try out various design strategies or even a potential toolset, if a choice is available. They could be produced as early as feasibility to provide a proof of concept. They are potentially useful in the business study when the high-level system architecture is produced. However, their most usual position is during design and build to try out an alternative design, if the one that was originally envisaged is not working as well as expected. This is often very late in the project and therefore they are the least used category of prototype.

9.4 GETTING EFFECTIVE FEEDBACK

How the various prototype categories are used will have an impact on how effective they are in their respective purposes. Time should be allowed for the users to consider what they are seeing and to comment. This is particularly true of the business prototypes, which are possibly rather fragile, with large holes that make it difficult for the users to try out themselves. It is not uncommon for a developer to demonstrate a business prototype too quickly for the audience to think through all the ramifications of what is being presented. No adverse comments are forthcoming and the developer goes on to refine the work on an unsound basis. The result is that later, when the users see the next stage, they appear to have changed their minds from the earlier session. Prototyping is a dangerous way of developing systems if the business knowledge of the users is not utilized to the fullest extent. Development just degenerates into coding before you know what you are supposed to be doing.

Usability prototypes should be given to the users to operate with as little steering as possible from the developers: they are not going to be able to sit beside all the users forever. By leaving the users to operate the prototype themselves, important areas of misunderstanding will arise. It is very useful to get the users to talk through what they are doing and why they have chosen a particular action. This will help the developers to understand where they can improve the presentation, navigation, etc.

Concerns are often expressed about raising user expectations through early production of usability prototypes. One 'advantage' of the usability prototype is that it may well fall over unexpectedly. Another way of keeping expectations within realistic terms is to make a prototype perform rather poorly by putting in wait states – so long as they are removed later. In fact, wait states are a good idea, as they can be used to slow a prototype down to its expected speed when in production, so avoiding potential disappointment later when the users compare the delivered system with what they used during development. This is especially important if a higher specification of machine is being used during development than the one available to most end-users.

One of DSDM's products is the set of prototyping review documents. These are not produced after the event. If a prototype is being demonstrated, the demonstrator should be supported by a scribe who notes down all the points from the users as they are raised. If the users are trying out a prototype themselves, they should write down their own comments as they arise, but this approach should only be used if a large trial is being undertaken. The best approach is to have a developer sitting beside the user, catching every comment as it is made. Every effort should be made to gain complimentary comments as well as the adverse ones. It is just as useful to know what should be kept, as it is to know what should be changed. At the end of the session, the comments should be gone through with the users and the relative importance of the comments noted as the basis for future development.

Users should have business scenarios that they work through when exercising any class of prototype. If these are not used, then the users can be so caught up in the prototype that they lose sight of what they are trying to assess. This is particularly true for users who are moving to a complex graphical user interface for the first time.

9.5 KEEPING CONTROL

If a major change to the requirements (rather than a refinement) arises during the development of a prototype, it should be immediately dealt with through the channels prescribed by the project. All refinements to the requirements should be recorded as soon as possible after they have been identified and certainly no later than the end of the timebox in which the prototype is being produced.

The use of prototyping clarifies the business needs, but can muddy the technical vision if prototyping activities are not controlled within the technical framework. The technical vision is the responsibility of the Technical Co-ordinator. No prototype should be allowed to deviate from the design that is in place, nor to be non-conformant with the standards that have been set either by the organization or the project. Before any prototype is built, the Technical Co-ordinator should inform the prototype builders of any system constraints that will apply to the work they are about to undertake, and should remind them of its place in the overall system architecture. If the prototype builders identify a 'better' way of doing something, they should check with the Technical Co-ordinator that it does not endanger other areas of the architecture. When the prototype is nearly complete, its detailed design should be checked by the Technical Co-ordinator and incorporated into the system architecture. If technical issues arise during prototyping that cannot be addressed in the timescale or are outside the remit of the prototype, they should be reported to the Technical Co-ordinator.

The use of the three-phase timebox of investigation, refinement, and consolidation will stop developers from tinkering round the edges. With a clear set of priorities to work to, they will not try to 'gold-plate' the prototype. Their attention will be focused on delivering what is really needed, rather than going down paths that they personally find interesting and challenging.

9.6 KEY POINTS

- The differences between the languages of the users and developers should not be underestimated.

- Prototyping helps to break down the language barriers. Prototypes provide a common language.

- It also ensures that the right system is being built – errors are trapped early in the process.

- DSDM prototypes evolve into the delivered system.

- Four categories of prototype are defined: business, usability, performance and capacity, and capability/design. They are used in particular phases of development.

- Evaluation of prototypes through demonstration or user trials needs to be carefully managed to ensure all feedback from the users is captured.

- Developers need to be kept aware of the technical aspects of the system during prototyping. The Technical Co-ordinator role has an important part in ensuring this happens.

Chapter 10

The Agile Professional

10.1 'NO MORE QUICK AND DIRTY'

In the early 1990s, rapid application developers had acquired a bad name for putting systems together without regard to the long-term enhancement and amendments that would be necessary. Many of the developers who did not conform to this image pretended that they were not doing RAD at all. The introduction of DSDM allowed these more professional IT staff to come out of the closet. They are now able to say that they are using DSDM, a recognized agile method. One member of the Consortium said that previously his small team had been nicknamed 'the seagulls', because they swooped down to pick the choicest IT developments and left a mess behind. Now they are respected and seen as having been at the leading edge, as DSDM is now the standard method for all the organization's IT development.

Additionally, IT staff can be certified as DSDM practitioners through a rigorous examination procedure. To qualify for this status, people must attend an accredited DSDM course, have demonstrated at least six months of DSDM work, have written a paper about a project in which they have participated, and undergone an oral examination to test their detailed understanding of DSDM. By demanding not only training, but experience and demonstrable understanding of the issues within agile development, the DSDM practitioner certificate is seen to be of value within the UK, and as DSDM grows internationally developers and project managers everywhere will be able to see the certificate as a means of demonstrating professionalism in a field which many view as just a means of cutting corners. Part III contains more information about training and certification.

10.2 SKILLS AND ATTRIBUTES

Whatever the methods used, almost every project that has failed has done so because of some issue related to the people involved. It is rarely the technology which creates the real problems; technological problems are hard, but are often more tractable than those relating to people. One could almost say that IT personnel thrive on technological problems, but they often find the softer issues more difficult to resolve.

DSDM professionals must not only be skilled in the technology they use, but they should also be effective communicators, who are responsive to the needs of the users in their team. Many developers are very focused on the technology and the improvement of their own technical skills to the detriment of their soft skills. Indeed, some IT staff should never be let near people outside their own domain. We have all met somebody in IT who is a genius at what they do, but who is unable to interact effectively with other people. Every member of a DSDM team must be able to work in a co-operative and collaborative way with all other members of the team.

Moreover, due to the small team structures in DSDM, there should be no clear delineation between the various IT roles. The DSDM developer will have a broader view than just analysis or design or programming. For instance, someone whose main skills are in programming must be able to see beyond the programming task to understanding the users' requirements and interpreting them into a computerized form. This means that they should be capable of some analysis and design, but will obviously require support from other members of the team as they grow their skill set. The DSDM team should contain all the necessary core skills for a project and some members will be stronger in one area than another. By working collaboratively, every developer's skills are strengthened by the presence of others.

All of the above can be summed up in the statement that nobody should be protective of their area of work, nor the products arising from it. DSDM developers should actively promote user comments. Nevertheless, it can be disheartening to show work to a user who then pulls it to pieces because it does not do what was asked for. The ability of developers to change their views quickly about what is required is essential in DSDM. Flexibility is the key. Some developers find the need for flexibility very threatening, while others flourish in the DSDM environment. The developer who is firmly embedded in a regimented way of working will not make a good agile developer.

Some organizations worry about the move to DSDM. They feel that their IT staff who have always worked in hierarchically managed projects to clearly defined specifications will not be able to move to the flatter management style and more flexible specifications in DSDM. Admittedly, there are some developers who do not take to the new ways of working, but in the many DSDM projects that have been undertaken by organizations used to more traditional approaches, there have been very few developers who have not made the transition. Some have taken to it immediately and others have taken a few months to acclimatize themselves. From our experiences, only a handful of developers have felt uncomfortable in the long run. The stumbling block for these individuals has usually been the customer contact. They have found it hard to have their prototypes rejected by users who are seen as being unable to make up their minds. These 'failures' usually exhibit a very high degree of the rigorous, logical thinking that is necessary in IT and therefore expect to see it in everyone they deal with.

10.3 SELF-MANAGEMENT

DSDM is a controlled process, but it does leave a lot of the controls to the individual team members to perform. For instance, the guidelines on configuration management provide a set of rules for the project to follow, but how effective it is in practice will depend strongly on the developers themselves. Hence, all the best practices that have grown within IT over the last few decades are still present, but they need to be seen as important by the individual rather than something which is imposed by IT management, the project manager, or the quality management system.

Some DSDM projects are very small indeed, with just one or two developers. Where this is the case, it is even more important that IT management can be sure that all the relevant controls are effectively applied. It can be very easy in such a small team to think that the controls in DSDM can be ignored. This is never the case: DSDM has defined the minimum to make the final system both usable and maintainable.

10.4 KEY POINTS

- DSDM is not a home for hackers.
- The practitioner certificate demonstrates professionalism in agile development.
- Developers should be 'team players' whose focus is not only on technological problems.
- DSDM practitioners should be quality-conscious and manage their work effectively.

Chapter 11

Extreme Programming (XP) in a DSDM Environment

11.1 COMPETING AGILE METHODS?

Extreme Programming is an agile method that is currently enjoying a growth in popularity. It is designed for small teams of two to ten programmers working in a very free computer environment alongside user representatives. The timescale of projects is short, with three-week 'iterations' resulting in thoroughly tested, deliverable code. Team meetings and testing are carried out on a daily basis.[1]

From this summary it can be seen why many organizations see DSDM and XP as competing methods for application development. This chapter hopes to show how XP can be integrated into a DSDM project lifecycle.

There are many similarities in the approach and underlying principles of DSDM and XP. The similarities include:

♦ Customer involvement in teams, though the customers are not as proactive in XP as Ambassador Users are in DSDM. For instance, DSDM expects Ambassador Users to create all user related 'documents' such as help text, manuals, etc.

♦ Frequent testing: XP demands that test cases are written before the code: this is similar to defining the acceptance criteria before building anything in DSDM – whether code or not. Here the difference lies predominantly in the level of formality that is required by DSDM. Some DSDM can have as simple criteria as 'all "must have" functionality is provided'.

♦ Incremental change.

♦ Rapid feedback mechanisms.

---

[1] For further information on XP see *Extreme Programming Explained* by Kent Beck.

- Fast delivery.

- Focusing on what can and should be done now.

- Small teams.

- Developers are expected to be multi-skilled (designers, programmers, and testers).

11.2 DSDM AND XP IN HARMONY

DSDM and XP are complementary. Their philosophies are totally compatible; the difference lies in their focus and their range of applicability. As a technique, XP is light on project controls, does not provide full lifecycle coverage and is difficult to scale to larger projects. On the other hand, DSDM is deliberately light on programming techniques and good practice, in order to keep it relevant in every environment. Combining the two gives a controlled project framework with robust programming practices.

Where they differ is that DSDM defines a lifecycle and a generic set of management and technical products, whereas XP promotes techniques for agile programming and testing. These XP techniques can be used within the DSDM framework to create the programming-related products.

While XP relies on collective responsibility within the team for the quality of what is produced, not all personnel will be sufficiently experienced and skilled to achieve this at all times. DSDM agrees that quality is the day-to-day responsibility of teams. However, the DSDM roles of Technical Co-ordinator and Visionary have the ultimate responsibility for the technical and business quality of what is produced, and can take some of the 'pressure' from the developers, testers, and users.

Because of the deliberate lack of clear responsibilities, XP works best for small projects. Indeed, DSDM is equally successful in small projects, but the roles and responsibilities defined in DSDM mean that it is more easily scaled up to larger developments.

11.3 SOME REQUIREMENTS UNIQUE TO XP

XP relies heavily on pair programming, i.e. two developers sitting side by side with one creating code while the other thinks about the overall design and testability of what is being developed. Where this works, it is an admirable solution to achieving constant review of code and design. Unfortunately, some programmers will find this way of working uncomfortable, constraining, and inhibiting creativity. However, when developers enjoy this style of working they become ardent advocates. Pair programming can certainly be used in DSDM timeboxes, however, it should not be imposed on a team where it would be counter-productive. DSDM teams should have the autonomy to determine their own activities and methods of working to achieve the objectives set them.

The XP principle of defining test cases before coding should fit into the DSDM framework at most stages of prototyping. While there is a chance it might be impractical or put too much constraint on early prototyping, e.g. during an investigative iteration, it would be in line with good practice in refinement and consolidation iterations.

XP demands a robust and fast development environment. All new code is to be integrated and all tests run one hundred per cent every few hours (at least once a day). In many development environments, this is unfortunately not feasible; builds take time and the testing tools and environments are not sufficiently advanced to achieve this level of testing capability. DSDM determines the approach to testing on a project-by-project basis in the testing strategy produced in the business study. If adopting an XP approach, care should be taken in ensuring a suitable technical environment.

11.4 KEY POINTS

- ◆ DSDM and XP aim to solve the same problem: delivering good systems in short timescales.

- ◆ XP focuses on the act of programming, which is treated very lightly indeed in DSDM.

- ◆ DSDM provides a controlling framework into which XP can be plugged.

Chapter 12

Technology Support

12.1 THE NEED FOR TECHNOLOGY SUPPORT

The technology used to visualize what the developers are thinking and to gain feedback from that visualization is the basis of much of agile development. However, it is not the total answer. The technology support for a controlled process does not lie solely in the easy generation of analysis and design models, screens, and code. If the process is to be controlled, then strong emphasis should also be placed on automated support for the necessary controls. Controls are an overhead on productive work, albeit a necessary one. Savings in effort can be made by automating the control of the status of, and access to, work products and in ensuring that they have been created correctly.

Agile developers are like any other developers: they find certain activities tedious, even though they see the necessity for them. They would much rather spend their time creating the solution than controlling it. So it is the control activities that are likely to be squeezed out of their schedules when they are under pressure to deliver. So what do developers find most boring? Ask any group of developers and documentation is number one on the list. So the ability to produce documentation 'at the press of a button' should be one of the elements of an agile support environment. Another area that does not enthral developers is configuration management. However, configuration management is of prime importance in an agile environment, where more things are being produced and changed at a faster rate than in a traditional method. The need for support in this area is obviously fundamental. It should be easy for the developers to place their work under configuration management as soon as possible and as often as they should, without causing them to slow down in their development activities. Testing also looms large as something which developers see as a necessary evil, but which would be a much more productive activity with tool support. The list goes on.

12.2 *DSDM SUPPORT ENVIRONMENTS*

The DSDM Consortium has a policy not to recommend specific tools. Many of our members are tool vendors and it would be invidious to compare one offering with another. Indeed it would be an onerous and awesome task, which is best left to organizations who specialize in providing impartial, third-party assessments of tools. However, some members have taken the messages in the DSDM online manual to heart and have moved or are moving their tools nearer to what is required by the framework.

DSDM has defined an agile tool 'nirvana'. It is an environment which will support the whole process from feasibility to implementation (including aspects such as reverse engineering for legacy code) with all the necessary controls as automated as possible (see Figure 12.1). It does not exist and it is unlikely that any one tool vendor will offer the fully integrated set. Indeed it is yet another cry for an IPSE (integrated project support environment), but one which is designed for DSDM projects. Such an environment requires integration at a number of levels:

◆ **presentation** to provide a common 'look and feel' across all tools;

◆ **data** so that all tools share the same repository;

◆ **control** so that one tool can notify and/or initiate actions in other tools;

◆ **platform,** in order to port the toolset from one platform to another.

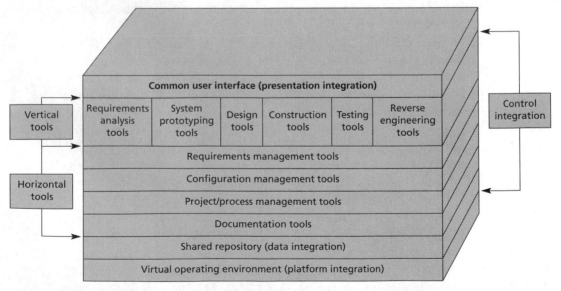

Figure 12.1 *An ideal support environment*

Maybe such an environment will exist in the future, but in the meantime we have to be more realistic and look for tools that will make savings in time and effort without being too costly. If we focus on the money side, several low-cost tools have been found to have a beneficial impact on effort. Low-cost tools for code and schema generation are available, as are tools for prototype generation. Both of these speed up development markedly compared with coding by hand. Another area where inexpensive tools can help is in the perennial headache of documentation. Automated support for creating documentation is readily available. Fortunately, many tools are self-documenting.

The ability to share information easily is also necessary. It can be of little value for one developer to produce an item, if it cannot be easily used by other members of the team. A repository is the solution to this. However, DSDM demands that it be a controlled repository. Developers performing different roles on a project should have different access rights to products and their variants and to products under construction. The access control should be automated to avoid abuse, whether intentional or otherwise.

12.3 TESTING TOOLS

One of the components of the DSDM support environment is testing tools. There are many varieties of testing tool available on the market and DSDM strongly advocates the use of tools in this area. Producing a tested system in a very short time can only be made easier with effective tools.

A very useful class of tools is capture and replay tools. These can lessen the need for documented test scripts. The quickest way to document tests is to record them as they are performed. A great deal of developer time can be saved through this route. Not only does this eliminate the need for producing 'paper' scripts before testing takes place, but the tests can be archived as evidence of what tests have taken place. Capture and replay tools are also extremely beneficial in building up regression test suites which can be left to run overnight while the developers have a well earned rest.

Static code analyzers can relieve the effort in code inspection and lessen the need for third-party verification that the code is to the required standard.

If the testing toolset is to be really complete, then dynamic analysis tools will perform tests in the background while demonstrations of a part of the software are taking place. Dynamic analysis includes checking array bounds and detecting memory leakage, etc.: things that should be tested, but which may be difficult to fit into the tight schedule of a project.

12.4 CONFIGURATION MANAGEMENT TOOLS

DSDM asks a lot of configuration management. Everything that is produced (analysis models, designs, data, software, tests, test results, etc.) should all be kept in step with one another, so that it is relatively easy to move back to a known 'build' state whenever the development has gone down a blind alley. This requirement means that automated support is essential and that the automated support should allow for many versions and variants. Ideally configuration management should be integrated into the tools used, but this is rarely the case (pardon the pun). Anyway, given the diversity of products that are under development at any one time, it is probably asking too much to expect all the relevant tools being used in a project to be sufficiently integrated to have every product in step. This means that a specialist configuration management tool should definitely be on the shopping list of an organization that is planning to take DSDM seriously. The ability to baseline everything on a daily basis is the ideal. So the tool should not incur too much of an overhead in its use. There are several excellent configuration management tools available which will do the job perfectly satisfactorily if the procedures governing their use are firmly in place.

12.5 EFFECTIVE TOOL USAGE

Although there are excellent tools on the market, any tool is only as good as its users. They should not be relied upon as the whole answer. The developers should be confident that they know how to use them properly and that the tools are an asset rather than otherwise. The purchaser of a tool environment for agile development should think carefully before buying. It is possible in early DSDM projects to live with what you already have. Indeed it is probably preferable not to introduce too many new things at the same time. Once the developers are used to the process, they will soon see where tool support would be particularly beneficial in their working environment. If tool support is to be bought, the purchaser should read the chapter in the online manual that gives very strong guidance on the characteristics of tools for DSDM. Not least of these is usability. For some reason, software tools are often less usable than their counterparts in the business environment – maybe we just like to make things hard for ourselves.

12.6 KEY POINTS

- ◆ Tool support is not just for producing technical products faster.
- ◆ Wherever possible, tools should be integrated.
- ◆ Tool support is particularly useful in testing, configuration management and the production of documentation.
- ◆ Do not buy tools specifically for DSDM until the organization has achieved a level of maturity in the application of the framework.

Chapter 13

Keeping the System Going

Despite its name, DSDM is not just about development. It can also be used as a framework for support and maintenance tasks after delivery of the solution. Some organizations have even stretched it to the limit and use it for IT infrastructure projects. This is hardly recognizable as DSDM, but it does conform to the nine underlying principles. The purpose of this chapter is to show how easily the principles of DSDM can be applied to maintenance activities, using a cut-down DSDM process. The benefit of this is that the strong business-centered focus is maintained throughout the life of a system.

Before going into the process it should be mentioned that the people expected to support the system are classified as Advisor Users during development. This means that they should be identified as early as the business study and involved as necessary in reviews, etc. during development: their agreement as to the maintainability of the product is one of the success criteria for a project. This involvement also means that they understand what the system does and are aware of the business case for the product, and its relative importance in the overall portfolio of systems, well in advance of it becoming their responsibility.

As is usual, the support and maintenance team classify all change requests as bug-fixes, enhancements, etc., and estimate the cost of each as they are received. If a change request requires urgent attention, it will naturally be dealt with immediately. Otherwise, the DSDM maintenance process would be used for a bundled set of change requests. Major enhancements will often warrant the use of the full DSDM development lifecycle.

It would be usual for the maintenance team to consist simply of a Team Leader, Developers, and Testers, with only occasional involvement from Ambassador Users. Generally the Team Leader will assume the responsibilities usually associated with the role of project manager within a DSDM development project.

Timeboxing Approach

To achieve a controlled approach to release management, every effort should be made to gain consensus between IT and business management for an agreed schedule of deliveries of system changes.

However, rock-solid timeboxing is unlikely to be achievable in a maintenance project because the team cannot be 'isolated' in the same way that they would in a normal DSDM development. It is in the nature of support and maintenance roles that staff will need to react to requests for immediate help on an ad hoc basis. Depending on the effort required for the immediate work, the changes that are being developed may have to be put on hold. Once the problem has been resolved, the maintenance team determine the impact on the work on hold and then agree with the relevant business managers any necessary alterations to the delivery schedule.

Setting the Priorities

A kick-off workshop is run to decide the scope of the next set of delivered changes – taking into account both business need and technical constraints. This means that the active participants must include line managers, acting as mini-Visionaries, from all relevant areas, Ambassador Users from the same areas and the support and maintenance team.

Based on the costs and business and technical needs, the scope of enhancements is agreed and prioritized using the MoSCoW rules.

The delivery date (or schedule of dates) is agreed. As with any timebox, if the delivery date is immovable, it is essential that not everything within the set of changes to be tackled is a 'must have'.

Having agreed the scope, prioritization, and delivery date(s), the maintenance Team Leader produces a detailed plan up to the delivery date (with any further delivery dates shown as milestones with little detailed planning between them).

For each delivery, Ambassador Users should be identified who can participate in decision-making during the maintenance work, and are given the responsibility for accepting work on an ongoing basis. This will almost invariably be at a much lower level of commitment than in a development team.

Delivering the Change

The changes are designed, coded and tested by the maintenance team. As in any DSDM work, the Ambassador Users should be involved in incremental testing and documentation of the change. They are also responsible for ensuring the user community is prepared for the change, for instance arranging for training and dissemination of updated documentation.

Any outstanding change requests at the delivery date are reviewed and the process returns them to the 'in-tray' of the support team. The process returns to the planning phase to confirm the contents and date of the next delivery of system changes.

13.1 KEY POINTS

- ◆ Support and maintenance staff must be involved in development projects from the earliest stages.

- ◆ DSDM extends beyond development projects into support and maintenance.

- ◆ User involvement is still required to ensure business relevance.

Part II

Case Studies

This section contains case studies of ten projects. All but one of the case studies were written by people from the projects under discussion. They are of varying depth of detail and breadth of coverage and represent what the authors feel were important aspects of their projects. Each one demonstrates at least one important aspect of the use of DSDM. They all speak for themselves, but the next few paragraphs give a flavor of what they contain.

The first case study (Chapter 14) is from British Airways who have mandated DSDM as the foundation approach for all their IT projects, be they pure technical infrastructure, mainframe application enhancements, or development using the latest technologies. The case study covers the introduction of DSDM into their e-business development environment and some of the business issues that they had to address.

The framework is used both by internal IS/IT departments such as British Airways and by many third-party suppliers. The second case study (Chapter 15) describes the latter: it shows how Syntegra successfully supplied the project management and development expertise to an important e-business project within Hitachi Europe, who provided the business knowledge that is fundamental to DSDM projects.

DSDM is a management philosophy embodied in a framework, with techniques that can be applied anywhere. The third case study (Chapter 16) describes how DSDM was used in a project with no IT content whatsoever. This should help the reader see how DSDM can become a 'way of life'.

Since DSDM is a framework, other methods and techniques can be plugged into it. Sometimes this can require a bit of thought. However, the use of UML (Unified Modeling Language) inside DSDM is easily achieved. The fourth case study (Chapter 17) shows how this works, both in theory and in practice.

Since DSDM is about collaborative working, it can be difficult to imagine how it would work with offshore development companies. Xansa have been using their offshore partners in DSDM projects with considerable success for some years. The next case study (Chapter 18) shows some of the changes that they have had to make to the base framework to achieve this.

The next case study, Chapter 19, is a miscellany of "war stories" describing projects that got it wrong. These are necessarily anonymous and high-level, but each brings out a potential pitfall for those coming new to DSDM.

The BT case study is the only one carried over from the first edition of *DSDM: The Method in Practice*. While it describes a project in considerable detail, the most interesting part of this case study is the graphs of various metrics of people's attitudes, etc., that were kept regularly throughout the project. The significance of some of the metrics will require careful inspection of the graphs in relation to the supporting text.

When DSDM becomes part of an organization's standard practice, it is often the case that they build some automated support tool, using technology from a simple database to a fully interactive process support environment. The case study in Chapter 21 describes a fairly simple tool, together with some of the lessons that Atos Origin learned during the introduction of DSDM. At the time of writing the 'DSDM Suitcase' tool is available via the DSDM website.

The BT case study measured people's attitudes to agile development, while the case study in Chapter 22 takes a formal and rigorous approach to measuring the process improvements brought by DSDM. A part of SchlumbergerSema in Sweden determined improvement targets and specific metrics to use in assessing their achievement, while running a pilot DSDM project. This case study covers both the pilot and the improvement activities. It also summarizes the improvements that clearly exceeded the originally planned targets.

The final case study is another example of how the flexibility of the DSDM framework enables other techniques and methods to be used with it, as in the case of UML. It shows how the business rules based methodology can fit into and around the DSDM lifecycle.

Chapter 14

Implementing DSDM in eBA

British Airways is a founder member of the DSDM Consortium. They decided in 1996 to spread the use of DSDM more widely across their IT department. It is now the default approach for all projects on all platforms from batch mainframe development through to small PC-based applications. This chapter discusses how DSDM was successfully introduced alongside setting up a new business area in 1999 to manage all BA's e-business.

The case study was written by Gwen Young, one of the group of consultants that British Airways brought in to assist with embedding DSDM into the corporate culture. Each consultant was aligned to a separate business area, e.g. cargo. Each area had its own set of problems to address; the case study's focus is e-business only.

14.1 INTRODUCTION

Anyone with access to the internet will no doubt have used its facilities to check or book travel arrangements. It was an obvious step for British Airways therefore to invest heavily in their website, www.britishairways.com, as well as developing a presence in other channels (iTV, WAP, etc). In the mid-1990s, e-commerce developments were seen as nothing special, so the existing IT and customer BA departments took on project work in much the same way as other projects were carried out.

14.2 CREATING eBA

These arrangements were unsatisfactory to the internal BA community on several occasions, due to the following characteristics of the projects:

1. time to market was crucial;

2. specialist IT skills were required;

3. marketing activities needed to be closely co-ordinated alongside the IT development.

In 1999, a new department was created, called eBA; its overriding objective was to push 50 per cent of BA's business online within two years. eBA staff were seconded from customer areas within BA for a two-year period. To service this department, a sister IT function was created, so expertise in the various channels could be cultivated.

14.3 INTRODUCING DSDM

Using DSDM was a 'no-brainer' decision for eBA. Customers and IT staff had used it in the past and were pleased with the outcome of the projects. The head of e-commerce promoted fiercely the concept of '90-day projects', which of course tied in nicely with DSDM concepts such as dividing projects into manageable increments and committing to a fixed end date. eBA were happy to state that DSDM was their 'method of choice', and would always be chosen unless the project had very peculiar characteristics.

14.4 eBA ROLES

There are two major roles within eBA dealing with the development of functionality on a channel:

♦ **Project lead:** this person is responsible for the overall project plan. They will manage the IT part of any project, as well as any marketing or sales activity that needs to go on alongside. They commit to a delivery date and an agreed set of functionality. This would equate to the DSDM project manager role.

♦ **Process and implementation lead:** this is very similar to the DSDM role of an Ambassador User. The process lead is aware of the requirements for the project, and involves other BA staff if appropriate. The process lead usually has sales or marketing experience. This is one of the ways eBA gets around the problem presented by e-commerce developments, which are your user community. The process lead may use focus groups or prototype trials with the general public to ensure requirements being passed on to the technicians are appropriate.

If all or part of the development is being undertaken by internal IT resources, a Technical Lead will be assigned. In all circumstances an Application Architect over-

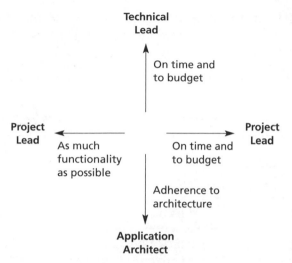

Figure 14.1 Roles with their differing responsibilities

sees the project, to ensure the e-commerce platform is being used in an optimum way (encouraging reuse, adherence to the standards, etc.). See Figure 14.1.

Overall, the roles have been created so that some healthy conflict will emerge on each project. For instance, it may take longer for a particular project to make a component reusable, it's up to the architect and technical lead to slug it out on each project.

14.5 REWARD SCHEMES

One interesting problem for eBA centered on how to implement a reward scheme. DSDM added extra complications to that problem. eBA staff were rewarded if they delivered a system:

1. on time (a given with DSDM);

2. to budget (over budget is possible at BA, even using DSDM, as flexitime can be used, but this is acceptable);

3. which meets a specific list of non-functional requirements (for example, a new online system does not generate more than 20 calls a week to the helpdesk);

4. meets an agreed set of functionality.

For the functionality performance measure, the MoSCoW list was used, and in most cases, the cut-off point for reward payment was all of the 'musts' and some of the 'shoulds'. This affected the ability of all projects to use MoSCoW effectively, as the project teams perceived the prioritized requirements list in a different way to the way it was agreed during business study (see Table 14.1).

Table 14.1 *Effect of Bonus Scheme on Original MoSCoW List*

	Original MoSCoW	**Perceived MoSCoW**
Requirement 1	must	must
Requirement 2	must	must
Requirement 3	should	must
Requirement 4	should	must
Trigger point for bonus payment		
Requirement 5	should	could
Requirement 6	could	could
Requirement 7	could	could
Requirement 8	won't	could

The tight timescales of all the projects meant that the bonus scheme agreements derived in business study were often not updated during the prototyping phase of the lifecycle. An additional problem was that the IT function had a slightly different reward scheme. Despite all of this, in general the reward scheme was perceived to be fair by eBA staff.

14.6 THE ENVIRONMENT

Team-building

Right from the word go, the management of the new department recognized that to get the best performance from the eBA teams, a great deal of investment should go into organizing occasional non-work activities. These activities would help eBA staff work well together, as well as ensuring they get at least some relaxation time between very intensive projects. Team building activities have included offsite, organized activities, as well as social events for the entire department or for smaller project teams to celebrate reaching a particular milestone.

Technique Coaching

Alongside the consultancy support for DSDM, a program began to enhance the knowledge of those in the IT section of eBA at the same time as developing and communicating some standards. Informal lunchtime lectures often incorporating some practical work were so popular with staff that their frequency and capacity had to be increased very early on in the schedule. Sessions covered subjects such as:

- translating business requirements into Use Cases;
- regression testing using internal and external resources;
- the BA e-commerce platform;
- effective use of the three DSDM prototype iterations.

Often, discussions at these sessions led to the publication of amendment of a standard, which was quickly bought in and applied, as everyone had been involved in its creation.

Another popular part of the technique-coaching program was the 'top tip'! Every few days, a handy hint or a piece of good practice was posted up on the coffee machine (where we know everyone goes at least once a day!). Not only did it mean fewer errors in coding or testing; it started knowledge sharing at the coffee machine, as technicians discussed related problems and solutions.

Typical Projects

Projects enter eBA for all sorts of reasons. A very common scenario is one where the marketing departments want to acquire more online relationships with customers, so a very short-term item may appear on the site, such as a competition/questionnaire. These projects have two very fixed end-dates: the date when the application must be loaded on to the site and the closing date of the competition after which all entry capabilities must be removed and the winner information publicized. Another typical project involves providing some services online which would ordinarily be carried out at the terminal building or by a call-center. In the past this has included arrival and departure information (updated every few minutes), booking, and loyalty scheme tracking.

DSDM Support

British Airways have employed a strong team of independent consultants for the past four years to assist with the implementation of DSDM. As eBA has so many fixed timescale projects, the consultancy team has always provided extra help. In the past year, there has been an initiative to get more eBA professionals through their DSDM exams. A target of three staff going for their DSDM practitioner exams in each quarter has been set. Consultants and other practitioners along with BA staff mentor the examinees. Help is given in the form of lunchtime topic sessions, as well as mock exams.

Project Readiness Reviews

Before a project enters functional model iteration, a panel of senior eBA and IT staff question the project lead and the technical lead on their readiness to deliver the project on time and within budget. On a DSDM project, this will include a review of high-level estimates in association with the MoSCoWed requirements. The panel will also ensure key personnel are in place and that issues such as reuse have been considered.

If the project can go ahead, risks identified in this review will obviously form part of the project lead's risk register.

Use of UML

Models are used extensively in the IT section within eBA. Much of the early technique coaching sessions concentrated on Unified Modeling Language (UML) skills. In the early days, the Business Area Definition was produced in a written form and application architects were responsible for producing UML models from that. Since then, some success has been achieved using a UML modeler in a facilitated workshop environment, to record business requirements.

14.7 EXAMPLE PROJECT

Account Status

We all know what Executive Club is, but what about onBusiness and Venture Club? Well, these are loyalty schemes for SMEs (small and medium-sized enterprises). Companies can earn points for flying on BA, and these can be redeemed for a host of wonderful gifts (table football has proven popular with the internet start-ups) and also redemptions can be made on flights. onBusiness is the UK scheme and Venture Club is for the USA and Canada.

Members of onBusiness and Venture Club receive a statement every quarter, detailing all transactions. In August 2001, a project was initiated in eBA. The proposal was to allow members of the schemes to get instantaneous updates on the web and also allow searching and sorting so a company can ask the question, 'Just how many points did I earn last year on my LHR–JFK flights?'.

The Business Study was conducted through a series of two- and three-day workshops in New York, as much of the data manipulation and web page design would be

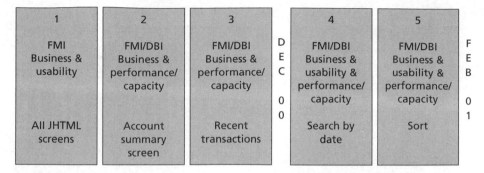

Figure 14.2 *The eBA project plan*

carried out by IT partners based in the USA. The final workshop derived a very successful project plan, where the 90-day project would be split up still further (see Figure 14.2).

The technical lead determined that things are going to get quite complicated when we introduce search and sort, e.g. what if you search and you bring back more than 200 transactions, what do you do about paging, etc. So, how about developing the ten most recent transactions first, and using that to ensure transactions are displayed okay, that can be delivered to the live site, then work can start on sort and search for a second delivery. The team came up with five timeboxes, and agreed the kick-off dates, as well as testing dates and review dates. In the same workshop the team got the detail for the first timebox, as this was going to be mainly web page deliverables, going through investigate, refine, and consolidate reviews with the Ambassador Users in a conference call.

In fact the project delivered earlier than the dates originally planned: the December deliverable was eight days early and the February deliverable came in January.

For more information contact either the author of this case study, Gwen Young, e-mail: gwen_young@yahoo.com or Caroline Barnsdall-Thompson, e-mail: caroline. e.barnsdall-thompson@britishairways.com.

Chapter 15

DSDM and Eliminating the Contractual Divide

In contrast to the previous case study, which was about using DSDM on internally sourced e-business projects, this case study describes Syntegra's use of DSDM on a key e-business project for Hitachi Europe. It outlines the market conditions for the project, business benefits, roles and personalities involved from both the customer (Hitachi) and supplier (Syntegra) side, details of the DSDM approach, and lessons learned.

15.1 INTRODUCTION

The aim of the eTechnology Pathfinder project at Hitachi Europe Ltd. was to provide a testbed for the rollout of a common e-business platform across Hitachi's 11 business divisions. Users were Hitachi staff and external customers.

The scope of Pathfinder, just a small part of the eTechnology programme, was limited to the rollout of a web-enabled self-service application for Hitachi's Digital Media Group (DMG), running on the new platform. This application would allow customers to track their orders 24/7.

At the time of Pathfinder, while the eTechnology platform featured prominently in Hitachi's IT plans, DSDM had not been rolled out across the business. Most Hitachi staff were unfamiliar with DSDM techniques, though some had experience of waterfall developments.

15.2 PROJECT LIFECYCLE

The overall timebox for the project was five months for setting up the eTechnology platform infrastructure, and three months for the development of the customer application. Within the overall timebox, lower-level timeboxes were scheduled, according to Table 15.1.

Table 15.1 Project Lifecycle

Timebox	Duration (weeks)	Activities
1	6	A drill-down workshop, at which the definition of the business area and systems architecture was agreed, took place prior to project kick-off. The first timebox started with a planning meeting, then a DSDM awareness presentation was given to all business representatives. This was followed by the first facilitated workshop at which the output from the drill-down workshop was reviewed, a high-level MoSCoW list agreed, and Use Cases, an initial storyboard, and first-cut data map were produced. While the initial infrastructure was being set up a throwaway prototype was developed, based on the output from the planning workshop.
2	4	The second timebox began with workshop I (at which the initial prototype was reviewed, more detailed functional requirements captured as a refined MoSCoW list, an initial non-functional requirements list produced, and a functional prototype reviewed). In addition the storyboard was refined and use cases consolidated. The initial functional prototype was built from the workshop output.
3	3	The third timebox began with workshop II at which the initial functional prototype was reviewed, further functional requirements were captured (again by refining the MoSCoW list), the storyboard refined, and a minor review undertaken of use cases. The second functional prototype was then developed from the workshop output, leaning primarily on the MoSCoW list, which was by now providing a robust definition of requirements.
4	3	The fourth timebox began with workshop III, at which the requirements were consolidated by agreeing the second functional prototype. Minor amendments to the requirements

Table 15.1 Continued

Timebox	Duration (weeks)	Activities
		were captured for the final deliverable and use cases were updated to be in line with the MoSCoW list. Following this the final application developments, producing the delivered CSS portal, were completed.
		Documentation of a full functional specification was produced from the workshop notes. Users were trained, and documentation was produced which included a trace of all requirements. During a project review meeting, the system was tested and the prototype reviewed.
		Further user acceptance testing was completed, then the CSS portal was delivered.

15.3 THE PROJECT

In 1999 Hitachi concluded that all its operations needed to be capable of conducting business electronically; to reduce administrative overheads, to continue to provide the excellent customer service for which the business is renowned, and to maintain strategic advantage in a market with peaks and troughs.

'Some of our suppliers and competitors had e-capability already, so we had to move quickly,' explained Mark Checkley, Business Solutions Manager for the Information Technology Group (ITG) at Hitachi Europe. 'Harnessing energy and ideas from within the business, we took the decision to build a common e-business platform that would support a range of web-based applications, to raise customer service levels and streamline our internal processes.

'One of the biggest challenges was doing this in a cost-effective fashion, so we opted for a single infrastructure whose cost could be leveraged across all 11 business groups.'

But Hitachi recognized that it couldn't undertake such a large-scale and business-critical IT program alone, and in early 2000 issued a formal invitation to tender (ITT). Mark describes Hitachi at that time as essentially a 'green-field' site. 'We had internet access and an intranet, but no e-capability; no hardware, software or skills in-house for electronic business.'

In May 2000 Hitachi selected Syntegra as their partner. Syntegra is a global consulting and systems integration business with experience of DSDM.

Mark said: 'With the technology platform we opted for a best-of-breed approach, starting small and scaling quickly. In the end we chose a standards-based architecture comprising Sun hardware and iPlanet software.'

Having gathered and prioritized the business requirements of all 11 groups, Hitachi commenced work on the eTechnology program with Syntegra in December 2000.

Mark Checkley explains: 'Two streams of work went on simultaneously: first, the rollout of the technology infrastructure that would underpin our entire e-capability, and second, the development and rollout of the first application to run on the platform; the customer self-service application (CSS) giving distributors and OEMs 24-hour access to their orders and delivery status via the web. This was collectively known as the Pathfinder project.'

15.4 APPROACH

Pathfinder was a testbed for the rollout of web-enabled self-service applications on Hitachi's new eTechnology platform. It included the rollout out of an entire new e-technology infrastructure across Hitachi Europe's 11 business units, integration to internal operational systems and those of third parties, and a customer order-tracking application running on the platform. This was therefore a hybrid project that would not necessarily have been suitable for DSDM.

DSDM works very well for the development of applications that are visible at the user interface, but in this project the ability to 'see' the final system was entirely dependent on the networking which supported the system, which in turn was dependent on the success of the integration with Hitachi's ERP system.

However, DSDM was chosen because Pathfinder passed the initial feasibility study, and because Hitachi was willing to trust Syntegra and learn about the framework despite having no prior experience of it. When Pathfinder was discussed, Syntegra had been working with Hitachi for three years, during which time the two organizations had demonstrated significant cultural fit.

In particular DSDM was felt to be suitable because of the extremely tight deadline for project delivery; Hitachi required rapid time to market to recover maximum business benefit and stay ahead of the competition. Furthermore the objectives and priorities of the business were destined to evolve and change during implementation.

Pathfinder complied with most of the DSDM suitability filter questions, though to comply fully Syntegra had to work fairly hard to persuade Hitachi that some of the 'no' responses to Suitability/Risk List questions could become 'yes' responses. Significantly, they had to persuade Hitachi to allow senior users to devote a considerable chunk of their time to the project.

Syntegra invested a lot of time prior to the start of the project talking to Hitachi about the benefits of DSDM. They discussed with the Visionary the 'cost' to the business of freeing up some very senior staff members, typically those most vital to operations. Syntegra advised Hitachi's Project Sponsor that it was important not to underestimate the time commitment required from key people and, after the initial persuasion, were delighted to get that commitment. Hitachi also recognized that with DSDM, they would be putting their people in an environment of continuous change for some time, and that change had to be managed.

The project team had varying levels of DSDM experience, so two DSDM awareness workshops were provided to bring all team members up to a common level of understanding. During and following DSDM awareness training, prior to the initial development workshop, Syntegra communicated to Hitachi the importance of empowering the team.

15.5 PERSONALITIES AND ROLES

In addition to the sponsoring group within Hitachi, DMG, plus ITG, Hitachi employed a third-party graphic design agency. Representatives from this agency attended the facilitated workshops, and provided PowerPoint slides and Flash demos for early prototypes.

There was also some discussion outside of workshop activity with representatives from a third-party logistics supplier whose information was to be accessed from the customer order tracking system. The roles described below remained constant for the duration of the project.

The Executive Sponsor was DMG's European sales operations manager. He was a strong advocate for the new system, and had the power to make decisions and secure attendance from key people. In addition to ensuring that funds and resources were made available, he was a strong and authoritative character who could make things happen. He also attended at least part of every workshop.

The Visionary was DMG's market and business planning manager, and a champion of the CSS portal. He was immensely enthusiastic and committed to the project and its business goals, and attended every workshop. The Visionary also provided a key channel of communication between Syntegra, Hitachi, and ABA Design.

The Ambassador Users were senior customer services staff, who were enthusiastic and driven to make the project succeed. Their background knowledge provided valuable input to the project.

The three Advisor Users from Hitachi and ABA Design contributed throughout the functional modeling iterations and the design and build iterations. One of the Advisor Users (from Hitachi), with exceptional knowledge of the legacy systems, later became involved in the development. Additionally, ABA Design provided Advisor Users who were also seen as developers due to their involvement in prototypes (see later).

The Technical Co-ordinator had more than ten years of industry knowledge, including DSDM, and provided strong technical skills in the iPlanet application. The Facilitator had more than 15 years' experience of agile methods, and 35 years' experience of systems development. The Developers were chosen on the grounds of their experience in e-business application development and integration.

15.6 FUNCTIONAL MODEL ITERATION AND DESIGN AND BUILD ITERATION

Prior to commencing the facilitated workshops, it was agreed that every member of the team should be empowered. This was evident in the workshops as everyone contributed and aired their concerns and ideas. This empowerment was only overridden on one occasion, as described later in this section. Ambassador and Advisor Users participated in all workshops and in testing and rollout.

Project initiation comprised four workshops, each followed by a fixed timebox, during which time the system was developed and refined iteratively. The length of the timeboxes was chosen to accommodate the extra time required for integration. The initial timeboxes had to be extended slightly because the hardware and software was being used for the e-technology infrastructure project, which was running concurrently to the CSS portal design.

The team worked around this by using PowerPoint and Flash demos to demonstrate prototype functionality in the early stages. Once the front-end had been integrated with Hitachi's legacy systems, they were able to demonstrate iPlanet prototypes.

The facilitated workshops defined and prioritized requirements using MoSCoW lists. At each workshop, the requirements list from the previous workshop was refined by reviewing the prototype, refining the storyboard, generating requirements for the new prototype, and updating the Use Cases. Use Cases helped the developers understand the business flow. Every attendee received a copy of the workshop outputs, thus allowing them to consider the requirements prior to and during subsequent workshops.

The MoSCoW prioritization at the end of each workshop soon became a successful process, despite some members of DMG wanting more 'must' requirements in the early stages. As the workshops progressed, however, and the group became increasingly familiar with DSDM and the need to be realistic when prioritizing, less resistance was faced.

A potentially difficult situation arose at the start of the second workshop, when the development team heard from a management review that a business requirement that had previously been prioritized by the team as a 'won't have' was definitely to be included. The team rapidly re-prioritized the business requirements in the second workshop, in order to turn the requirement from a 'won't have' into a 'must'. This involved giving other requirements a lower priority, such that some 'shoulds' became 'coulds'.

At this juncture, Syntegra was very impressed with the maturity of the group in dealing with this tricky situation. In part, this maturity could be attributed to the extensive training in the DSDM approach before workshops commenced, and the spirit of the teams. Once familiar with DSDM, the team knew they could not at any point gain one requirement as a 'must', without dropping an equivalent requirement further down the priority list. The relationship between ITG, the Syntegra development team and DMG was highly collaborative, despite geographical constraints and differing priorities. Individual team members were based at separate sites in the UK: in Maidenhead, Fleet, Brighton and Newcastle, and the final system was hosted in Poole.

One way in which Pathfinder did deviate slightly from classic DSDM, was in testing the system extensively at the end of the project as well as during the design and build iterations. To accommodate the views of external users who had minimal involvement in the workshop process, and to test the complete integration of all the systems, Hitachi requested that Syntegra incorporated a fourth timebox for 'user acceptance testing'.

A working system was delivered within Pathfinder's five-month timeline; however, one of the team members did suggest that without the integration issues, they could probably have delivered the CSS portal in around three months.

Since this was a web-based system, with an infinite number of people potentially accessing the system at the same time, Syntegra also attempted to 'break' the system with rigorous performance testing.

15.7 THE BENEFITS

The Pathfinder project moved to go-live status after just five months in development, on 25 April 2001, within time and budget. The CSS application was a big success, with Hitachi's customers reporting a significant increase in satisfaction. Previously Hitachi distributors were not able to track orders in an efficient or simple way.

Hitachi also experienced considerable internal benefits. Customers could access information much faster than over the phone, but also Hitachi's customer service staff were able to spend more time on value-added tasks rather than constantly answering queries.

Since the success of Pathfinder, Hitachi has rolled out several other web-based applications.

15.8 LESSONS LEARNED

Where DSDM is not a company-wide standard, it is vital to train the team members in DSDM immediately prior to project commencement. With Pathfinder the first training session took place the day before the first workshop, so minds were fresh and on track. This paid dividends when the team had to re-prioritize project requirements in the second workshop; they recognized immediately that in order to accommodate a late requirement, they had to lose an existing one to avoid growing the scope of the project.

Crucially Hitachi learned that DSDM was a good thing, as it gave them a firm handle on what was going on, and ultimately delivered the system their customers wanted, within the desired timeframe. They were somewhat surprised initially at the amount of detailed planning that went into the workshops, particularly by the facilitator, but were pleased with the end results.

Version control was an issue early on in the project, particularly between the two parties, but better version control management emerged as the project progressed.

Occasionally it was also difficult to secure the attendance of every individual for the duration of every workshop, but the team found that better attendance was achieved through agreeing ground rules for workshop etiquette at the outset. These rules are intended to set out acceptable behavior during a DSDM project, and to embrace and accommodate cultural difference. Syntegra also discovered it was sometimes easier to enforce attendance as a third party than it would perhaps be as an internal member of staff.

One of the major sticking points Syntegra has found with DSDM projects surrounds the prompt sign-off of workshop notes to declare they are a hundred per cent accurate and a true representation of workshop content. It can be a very sensitive issue, even when the partnership between the two companies is strong.

Hitachi appreciated the need to sign off notes rapidly, and got quicker at this as the timeline progressed, allowing the team to proceed quickly from one workshop to the next.

Finally Syntegra learned a very valuable lesson concerning when and where to use Use Cases. In their view, users prefer to use MoSCoW lists to describe their requirements, whereas object-oriented developers prefer Use Cases because it gives them more of a clue as to how to build the system. At the outset, they began by creating MoSCoW lists first, then tried to build Use Cases from the requirements lists in the workshops with users. However, they quickly switched to a different way of working on discovering that users were getting bogged down with Use Cases; they asked the Technical Co-ordinator to build all the Use Cases prior to subsequent workshops, and on future projects they plan to use Use Cases that they have prepared earlier, to speed up progress still further.

For more information, contact Linda MacCallum-Stewart at Syntegra-UK, Spitfire House, 141 Davigdor Road, Brighton BN3 1RE, East Sussex, UK. Tel. +44 (0)1273 762500. E-mail: linda.maccallum-stewart@syntegra.com.

Chapter 16

DSDM in a Non-IT Project

While DSDM was conceived and started in the UK, it is increasingly international. The second Consortium to be set up was DSDM Benelux. This case study demonstrates the maturity that has been reached by Dutch DSDM practitioners since it takes DSDM beyond IT into the wider business community. Peter Coesmans is Chair of DSDM Benelux.

16.1 INTRODUCTION

This example handles the successful use of DSDM for a project that had absolutely nothing to do with IT. It shows that for this project, the use of a DSDM-type approach was absolutely crucial in order to achieve success. Moreover, it shows that DSDM is suitable for a variety of projects much wider than IT-related projects. Special attention is given to the functional model iteration workshop in which three iterations were delivered in three days.

16.2 THE ENVIRONMENT OF THE PROJECT

A very large construction and building company had found out that while their core business was to deliver projects successfully, the level of project management in the company was not as it should be. To achieve this, a competence program was started that addressed enhancing project management competencies of various employees; incorporated project management as a career within the company valued equal to general management; defined a project management standard and created a project management office (PMO).

The construction company had hired P2 managers, a professional project management company, to run the program and also to provide the knowledge and competencies necessary. The program therefore, was run as a joint operation between P2 managers and the construction company.

After six months the momentum of the program had almost gone. While the career part of the project was going quite well, the other projects suffered from lack of enthusiasm. The development of courses, coaching, and mentoring in project management (skills enhancement) had come to a standstill. This project was chosen to re-energize the entire program by delivering good results fast. The decision was made during the summer holiday, by November that year an entire pilot series of tailor-made courses was to be run. Development started the second week of September, immediately after the summer holidays. A DSDM approach was chosen because:

◆ The desired result was a series of courses, mentoring, and coaching. There was no concept yet of how many courses or how many training days. It wasn't clear whether coaching and mentoring would be done by external (experienced) or internal (inexperienced, thus had to be trained) people. In summary: requirements not fixed.

◆ The construction company had to feel real ownership for the developed products.

◆ Quick delivery was of the essence, an incremental approach was possible.

◆ There was a sense of urgency to support the entire program with fast, high-quality results.

After running through the Suitability/Risk List successfully, the project was continued.

16.3 THE PROJECT

Feasibility/Business Study

Reports similar to the Business Area Definition, System Architecture Definition and Development Plan were created. The Business Area Definition showed the target audience for the development program, which holes there were in current knowledge and which desires the company had with respect to the subject. Of course there was also a first-cut Prioritized Requirements list!

The System Architecture Definition showed the approach to learning, which standards to use, which deliverables made up a 'course', how much time in what type of course should be used for practical and how much time for theoretical work, etc. It also showed where mentoring and coaching fitted into the entire development program – in between or next to courses – thereby on a high level defining the proposed solution.

These phases were done over the summer holidays. Much was done to gain support in the construction company for the approach and make sure the right people supported this initiative through commitment and involvement. Much effort was put into preparations to regain momentum as soon as the holidays were over:

- enlisting people for the development teams;

- gathering as many materials from other, previous, proven courses as possible (reuse!).

Organization

The program manager acted as executive owner for the project, and the program sponsor was also the Executive Sponsor for this project. There was a (very DSDM experienced, accredited) project manager running the project, assisted by an experienced consultant in learning and training as Technical Co-ordinator and a senior manager from the construction company as Visionary. During functional model iteration and design and build iteration, there were three development teams running in parallel, with a central production office/secretariat supporting all three teams. Every team consisted of one or two Ambassador Users from the construction company, one or two project management experts from P2 managers and one or two independent project management trainers hired by P2. The project management expert in the team acted as Team Leader. Each team therefore had members to define the requirements, members having knowledge and skills, and members with experience in building courses from those knowledge and skills. All team members were only partially assigned to the project (1–3 days per week), and were located all over the country so had no shared room during Design and Build. A flexible attitude (traveling, working hours) by all over a short period of time (six weeks) helped to overcome this problem. In total, those involved were four external trainers, three project management experts, six Ambassador Users, and five Advisor Users. During functional model iteration, three more project management experts and one more trainer (a specialist in soft skills) were present as experts.

Functional Model Iteration

In order to gain momentum, this phase was done in one giant workshop lasting for three days (and nights) in which three iterations were delivered. By the end of this workshop, it was clear which courses would be developed, what would be in them, a detailed time schedule for these courses, a first draft of teachers' notes and also the Implementation Plan. Moreover, the role of coaching and mentoring in between courses was described and was postponed to a later increment. Table 16.1 shows a high-level definition of the program which was agreed upon by everyone.

Since this workshop proved to be crucial for the success of the project, details are provided in a later paragraph. The program is now running successfully for its third consecutive year.

Table 16.1 *Training Program Definition*

Target audience	Name and form	Duration	Goal
Project leaders (1–3 yrs experience)	Operational project management course	2*2 days	Candidates have knowledge of project management essentials
	Project management mentoring on the job	At least 1 day a month	Candidates have experience with project management essentials
Project Managers (3–6 yrs experience)	Organizational project management course	2*3 days	Candidates have in-depth knowledge of project management techniques, principles, and skills
	Project management coaching	At least 1 day a month	Candidates show mastering of project management techniques and skills
Senior Project Managers and Project Directors (>7 yrs experience)	Strategic project management course	4 * 1.5 days	Candidates can master most problems that occur in large complex projects
	Project management board	1 day every 3 months	The 'masters of project management' meet regularly to review the status of project management within the company

Design and Build Iteration

The three teams built a new prototype of the courses every two weeks, which was tested by the Ambassador Users and reviewed sometimes by Advisor Users. The people from the central production office handled possible conflicts between courses. They also took care of configuration and version management of the materials. All slides, teachers' notes, practical materials, handouts etc., were produced up to the standards required. Also, the teams provided content for flyers and promotional materials.

After six weeks, a concluding workshop of one day was organized in which all teams presented the results and possible conflicts between courses were handled. All courses were presented and the entire group of people involved applauded the results. The Executive Sponsor gave all people involved a personal reward. The success of the project was published widely. After a preparation time (by project management) of four weeks, the entire project had delivered all results from scratch in seven weeks and was well within the projected costs. Reaching this first result was a big boost for the entire program.

The communication office of the program, also responsible for the internal marketing strategy, had created draft versions for the promotional materials, which looked stunning. They really provided the icing on the cake; the program was ready to roll.

Implementation

Operations such as enlisting delegates, producing materials, and assigning teachers now had to be put in place. Also the commercial side of the operation, getting project managers as delegates (or having their bosses assigning them) had to get up to speed fast using the developed internal marketing strategy. Within two weeks, the first course started, and within another four weeks, three more courses were successfully delivered. The momentum was really back in the program with this successful DSDM project. The other projects were finished successfully because they could use the slipstream of the motion created by this full-speed project.

16.4 *MAINTENANCE/POST-PROJECT*

After delivery, exceptionally low maintenance has been necessary for the courses. Some details were changed, but the courses still successfully meet the goals set for them at the opening workshop. In a second increment, successful mentoring by peers and coaching by project management professionals was put in place.

16.5 *THE FUNCTIONAL MODEL ITERATION WORKSHOP*

The functional model iteration workshop was crucial to the success of the initiative. The workshop was planned during summer holidays, and had to be conducted before the big projects would start again. Moreover, during the workshop the approach had to be proven and confidence in the entire program had to be regained. Careful planning and skillful facilitation took care of this.

The project manager, an experienced and accredited facilitator, ran the workshop. To overcome the 'two hats' problem, the Technical Co-ordinator stepped in as substitute project manager.

The session was planned in a hotel in the middle of nowhere, so everyone stayed day and night and was away from their usual work. Even mobiles didn't work.

Because of the timing, most participants only knew the goal of the workshop, how long it would take, and why they were there. These were going to be three days with 27 people working under high pressure.

The first morning, therefore, was used to get everyone up to speed on the information in the Business Area Definition, System Architecture Definition and Development Plan, to do some team-building, and to discuss ground rules and the way in which we would proceed. A first draft total program was created by the entire audience and teams were assigned for the afternoon to come up with a first version of the different products: goals for the courses, expected audience, expected length, work forms, etc. By the end of the afternoon of the first day, the draft program was agreed upon and all courses on a very high level were accepted (iteration 1). After a short break, a first draft time schedule outlining subjects and practical exercises was created. Then we had a late dinner and a good session walking around, bowling, swimming, and having a good time at the bar.

The second day, the experts were flown in and by the end of the morning the draft time schedule for all courses (iteration 2) was presented. After many discussions, iteration 3 was started, in which the materials gathered beforehand (slides, exercises, etc.) were assembled together with newly designed materials to form a first prototype. The production office (available on the spot) proved to be invaluable in finding the materials, creating new ones, gathering materials from the internet, etc. The second evening, after another late dinner, there were still some discussions on how to do risk management at 2 a.m. in the bar!

The last morning, all results were presented (iteration 3) and accepted (complete with Review Records). The afternoon was spent on issues such as naming the courses, the Implementation Plan, risk analysis, the position and style of mentoring and coaching, and how to continue in general. By the end of the afternoon, everyone was satisfied and very tired.

Prototyping had been done mainly horizontally, and gradually the courses were developed. Some modules were tested vertically though in the same time. What prototyping tools were used? PowerPoint, Word, computers, printers, a link to the internet and the P2 managers network, and some floppies.

16.6 CONCLUSION

The project delivered high-quality results in a very short period of time. The second increment was delivered when needed, six months later, by another team. The program regained enough momentum. The enthusiasm of the people from the building company who were involved spread fast over the entire company so that the program could be concluded successfully. First results from the program, cheaper and better managed projects (with respect to risks), were shown six months after the delivery of the first increment.

DSDM was the way to make this project a success. DSDM was not followed rigidly, but all products were delivered, the phases were followed, the organization, even the principles (where applicable) were fully there. Using this approach in a traditional project management (waterfall) environment was only possible because both project manager and program manager understood the need and knew what they were doing. The Executive Sponsor trusted them with this 'new' approach.

DSDM (or rather a DSDM-type approach) has been applied to several non-IT related projects by the author and his colleagues. The one described here was quite easy to relate to DSDM, but also in organizational development projects and in infrastructure projects (try building a road with DSDM...) using part of DSDM has been very beneficial. Sometimes the translation of 'prototypes', 'System Architecture Definition', and so on was not straightforward. Try timeboxing an organizational change (and guarantee delivery of the 'musts')! Working from the mindset of DSDM (the principles) and using the right tools from its toolbox gets many difficult projects successfully done.

For more information, contact Peter Coesmans, of P2 managers, Rosmalen, The Netherlands. Tel. +31 73 521 8222. E-mail: p.coesmans@p2managers.nl.

Chapter 17

An Object-oriented DSDM Project

In this chapter, Steve Ash covers both the theory and a practical example of integrating object-oriented techniques and notations with DSDM. The project story clearly shows how this can be achieved but, as this was a real project, not everything went perfectly and some issues are highlighted at the end of the chapter.

17.1 INTRODUCTION

There are many that believe that the concepts of object-oriented analysis, design, and implementation are incompatible with the principles of DSDM. This belief is difficult to understand in that object-oriented technology makes it straightforward to develop systems incrementally within a given software architecture.

This case study will describe a DSDM project concentrating on how the object-oriented products were produced and what impact the decision to use object orientation in a DSDM environment had.

17.2 THEORETICAL COMPATIBILITY OF OO/UML WITH DSDM

Since Ivar Jacobson's OOSE[1] and latterly the Unified Modeling Language (UML),[2] object-oriented analysis has started by decomposing the proposed system into Use Cases, which, for our purposes, can be considered to be Business Processes with

---

[1] *Object-Oriented Software Engineering.* 1992, Ivar Jacobson *et al.* Addison Wesley.
[2] Unified Modeling Language Version 1.3, Object Management Group (OMG). 2000.

which the System will give some help. This fits in well with the DSDM Business Area Definition purposes:

- To identify the business needs that should be supported by the proposed computer system.

- To outline the information requirements of the business processes that will be supported.

- To identify the classes of users impacted by the development and introduction of the proposed system.

- To identify the business processes and business scenarios that need to change.

- To clarify all interfaces with other systems (human or automated).

Object-oriented design basically consists of selecting an architecture (normally multi-tier), the communication protocols between the tiers, a management strategy within the tiers and suitable languages with which to build the tiers. Again, this fits in well with the System Architecture Definition purposes:

- To provide a common understanding of the technical architectures to be used during development and implementation.

- To describe the target platform and (if different) the development platform.

- To give an outline description of the software architecture (i.e. the major software objects or components – both process and data – and their interactions).

Object Technology enables ease of developing the required code incrementally; object orientation concepts encourage the development of small, reusable class operations/methods, which can be added to as required even after the class has been deployed.

17.3 PROJECT MOTIVATION

The project, a Point-of-Sale (POS) application for a thousand field salesmen, was originally conceived as a waterfall project as the first stage of a major downsizing from a mainframe system. The analysis and design were meant to provide the basis for later sales analysis and customer support systems.

The application was to enable the salesmen to sell one or more of six products with an average of six variations within each product and many cross-product selling rules dependent on the variations chosen.

The decision to use object orientation was taken at this stage more as a result of the chosen database software and associated development environment rather than from any potential medium- to long-term benefits of object orientation.

A 'full' feasibility study had been done (lasting three months) that interestingly included a prototype designed to obtain 'buy-in' from the wider user community.

It was at this stage that a major government regulatory decision was taken that meant the company had to be able to demonstrate an auditable sales process with the customer within six months. This was well inside the estimate already made by the chosen software house; a waterfall development contract had already been given.

In order that the essential elements of the new point-of-sale application be in place by the required time, the software house advised that the company adopt DSDM principles; if these elements were not in place the company was faced with a significant loss of income.

So, the focus of the project changed from providing the basis for management information to an auditable sales process.

17.4 FEASIBILITY STUDY

As already mentioned, a full 'waterfall' feasibility report had been produced; running through the Suitability/Risk List indicated no major foreseeable problems although the Additional Questions did indicate three areas of high risk. However, none of these risks involved the use of object orientation.

UML and DSDM training was given to all the developers, both from the software house and company; no users attended the training.

17.5 BUSINESS STUDY

Business Area Definition

Initially, it was planned to construct Use Case Diagrams in order to capture those processes that the application would have some help with. However, the one user available at the project re-launch and some company developers were uncomfortable with this approach and were sceptical that the diagrams would be complete enough to allow effective prioritization. A 'conventional' business process modeling exercise was undertaken, and the elementary business processes were mapped one-to-one to Use Cases that were then used to construct the Use Case Diagrams.

System Architecture Definition

During this process, the two technical architects modeled the tiers and chose the tier communication protocols. This was done using Package and Component

Diagrams – using a software drawing application because the chosen CASE Tool did not support these UML diagram types.

The architecture chosen was to have 'thin' user interface elements communicating with a business object layer, which in turn accessed the database via an object data access layer. Because the application was to reside on single laptop machines the inter-layer communication would be via that built in to the chosen development environment.

In addition, a communication protocol and technology was chosen for the data replication and headquarters database update; the responsibility for building this part of the system was to be outside of the scope of the POS project, but with an obvious dependency.

Although the resulting architecture could have been implemented without the use of object-oriented technology, object-orientation principles of encapsulation, and non-cyclic dependencies were the driving factors for the work.

It was at the end of the business study that the database designers on the team realized that a full database schema would not be available until late in the project because the database requirements were to be discovered incrementally. This would have caused problems outside of the project because the database schema was due to be an input to another project as part of the larger downsizing development program.

After much explanation and discussion, it was decided that the company would provide extra resource to design the database schema, taking the output of the first increment's business study and functional model iteration as a starting point and building on that from user input; this exercise was not part of the POS project. It was explained and 'understood' that the schema would probably have to change as the project progressed.

Prioritized Requirements List

The Prioritized Requirements List was based on the discovered Use Cases and the Development Plan was constructed with the needs of building the architectural components and the Prioritized Requirements List in mind. It was initially decided for the first increment to build the ability to sell one product end-to-end; however, the estimate for the 'musts', 'shoulds', and 'coulds' for this increment was approximately eight weeks' elapsed time.

One of the technical requirements was for data replication between a central database and the laptops; as this was essentially a requirement to fulfill the original MIS requirement, it was de-scoped from the first increment and the estimate reduced to six weeks.

Development Plan

There was a team of four business analysts and eight developers assigned to the project, so it was decided to run three concurrent increments at a time.

17.6 FUNCTIONAL MODEL ITERATION

The approach taken for the functional model iteration was to develop the textual descriptions for the selected increment Use Case and produce the Usability Prototypes iteratively. The textual descriptions were developed using structured English and documented as part of the Object Sequence Diagrams for each Use Case; this was done in an attempt to reduce the time it would have taken to map the more usual prose Use Case descriptions to that required for Object Sequence Diagrams. The Object Sequence Diagrams were built iteratively, in an essentially parallel exercise, with the prototypes.

From the Object Sequence Diagrams, a Business Class Diagram was developed from which the Logical Data Schema was abstracted; the Object Sequence Diagrams also formed an essential input to the design and build iteration.

Timeboxing techniques were used, with the documentation/modeling standards set as a 'must'; only business functionality was allowed to vary. Within the timeboxes, time was allowed for daily meetings between the concurrent increment developers in an effort to ensure consistency in the models and reduce duplication. Even though all teams were building the same overall model within the CASE tool, an early audit proved to the teams that these meetings were necessary.

There was a lack of user availability during the functional model iteration (see Section 17.9, Problems, below) so the prototyping and modeling sessions for an increment had to be carefully co-ordinated with those for the other concurrent increments.

It became clear during the first increment's functional model iteration that text alone would be insufficient to describe and understand the complexities of the product selling processes. Therefore, Product Sales Session State Models were constructed, the common pathways being refactored out into separate models for later reuse. The UML Activity Diagram type would have been a better medium for this documentation, but was not supported by the chosen CASE tool.

During the first increment's functional model iteration, two developers were tasked with producing a Capability/Technique Prototype to confirm the decisions documented in the System Architecture Definition and in an effort to reduce the time required for the first design and build iteration.

17.7 DESIGN AND BUILD ITERATION

Design and Build activities consisted of taking the models produced during the functional model iteration and modifying them in line with the requirements of the System Architecture Definition and the Capability/Technique Prototype. The results of the exercise were then incorporated into the prototypes.

There had been a great deal of time spent auditing the products of the functional model iteration and although this was resented by some early on, the ease of Design and Build proved the value of that activity during the functional model iteration stage.

There were two interesting object-orientation philosophy debates that arose at the beginning of the first design and build iteration:

Database stored procedures

It had been decided to sub-contract the database design and build to a third-party company specializing in the particular RDBMS chosen. The developers from this company stated that they required all the business rules so that these could be coded into the database stored procedures. These business rules had been documented as part of the class operation descriptions, and the chosen architecture called for object data requirements to be channelled through data access objects.

The advantage of this chosen architecture is to de-couple the applications from the database so that it is an easier task to maintain applications as the database structure changes; which was what was planned. Also, by keeping application data access in a well-defined layer within the application, future major database changes, e.g. change of supplier, move to distributed data, etc., are easier to cope with.

One of the major disadvantages of coding business rules into stored procedures is that the languages are relatively primitive; the resulting code is difficult to maintain (one reason why database administrators still seem reluctant to embrace change).

Multi-tier architecture

The chosen development environment made it very easy to develop a two-tier architecture (user interface and database), which was very useful when developing the user interface prototypes. The developers had a lot of experience in developing to this architecture and were at first uncomfortable about moving the business rules and application control elements to a middle layer. Their arguments about the potential extra time to develop were countered by explaining the areas of reuse within the project already discovered from the modeling exercises and the potential for reuse outside of the project.

Once this had been explained, the developers became generally enthusiastic with the approach; by the time of the first rollout, even the latent scepticism had disappeared.

17.8 IMPLEMENTATION

Because of the long lead-times for the hardware procurement, the early increments could not be implemented. This had the following effects on the DSDM recommended products:

User Documentation

There was a greater than normal amount of time to produce the online help system.

Trained User Population

There was a greater than normal amount of time to organize user training. This was considered to be a major advantage to the project in that it was possible to rollout the application to the majority of salesmen at once. It was considered that there was significant business benefit doing this rather than rolling out to widening groups of users as would have been necessary for normal incremental implementation. However, this strategy did mean that there was a greater amount of initial feedback to contend with.

Delivered System

There were two major effects although neither were object-orientation issues:

1. Early feedback from live use was not available and led to a longer first maintenance period.

2. The client company had a large testing department which insisted in being involved prior to implementation. It was advised that personnel from this department be 'seconded' to the project in order to ensure/do the required testing throughout the development. However, this was not acceptable, so normal DSDM testing was carried out and the increments delivered to the testing department so they could test again. Interestingly, only very minor comments were ever fed back.

One object orientation issue did occur with the testing department. Using 'Design by Contract', encapsulation, and de-coupling principles of object-oriented design and implementation, if a change in class code is required, but its public interface remains the same, the new code only has to be tested once; i.e. if it works once, it will work every time. However, the testing department insisted that full integration testing be done after every change; no problem was ever found.

If the increments were to be deployed as they were developed, this extra testing time would have delayed business benefit.

17.9 PROBLEMS

Apart from the problems already dealt with above, the following were the major problems encountered during the project.

Senior Management Understanding

The end-client senior management were given a half-day awareness training soon after it was decided by the IT Director to adopt DSDM for the project. All seemed enthusiastic but, as the project progressed, more and more requests for inappropriate (waterfall) documents were made. Initially, extra resource was procured to produce these documents and the project team was unaffected.

However, requests were made which indicated a lack of understanding and would have seriously compromised the DSDM philosophy. A further half-day awareness session for senior management was authorized by the IT Director which showed that although the general approach was understood, the day-to-day effects were not.

With the help of the IT Director, who was the DSDM Champion, senior management were persuaded to take a much more background 'advisory' role.

Contractual

One of the origins of the above problem was that the contract originally let with the outsourcing company was waterfall-based with appropriate deliverables agreed to. When DSDM was adopted, there was such strong motivation to get going that the contract was not re-negotiated. Therefore, senior management was trying to keep the outsourcing company to their now irrelevant contractual obligations.

User Availability

Despite being promised that four salesmen would be assigned full-time to the project, initially only one was available for 2–3 days per week, only becoming available after the formal training. This caused serious delays with the business study and the first increment's functional model iteration.

After the business study, this lack of user availability was fed into the estimates and the requirements re-prioritized. The revised estimates and prioritization indicated that the development team could only guarantee that the application would be able to support two of the six products in the given timescale. This fact was fed back to the Executive Sponsor and a further two salesmen were assigned; one full-time and the other 2–3 days per week.

17.10 CONCLUSION

At the end of the six-month timebox the application was deployed enabling salesmen to sell products which made up 90 per cent of the company income; approximately 75 per cent of the total portfolio. It is interesting to note that when a feasibility study was done for the ongoing development of the POS, it was decided to discontinue 10 per cent of the portfolio's remaining 25 per cent.

As a consequence of the project, although the testing department was retained for the waterfall projects, for future DSDM projects staff were seconded to the development teams as full-time members.

For more information contact Steve Ash, OO Training & Consultancy. E-mail: steve@ootac.com.

Chapter 18

How DSDM can De-risk Offshore Working

Xansa are keen advocates and users of the DSDM framework, as shown by the fact that, at the time of writing, the international Chairman and the Director responsible for training and accreditation worldwide are both Xansa employees. The company has been using offshore development capability for some years. They have developed the DSDM framework to manage the issues that such a distant partnership brings about: this case study describes some of the problems and solutions.

18.1 INTRODUCTION

The effective use of offshore resources is becoming increasingly important. Hilary Cropper, Executive Chairman of Xansa (a business consulting, information technology, and outsourcing company) stated, 'Service companies will die unless they use offshore development to cut their costs. If companies don't have that capability they won't survive. The fact that you can produce high-quality people at a fraction of the UK cost is key.'

18.2 CHALLENGES OF MANAGING AN OFFSHORE PROJECT

Offshore teams can provide cost-effective solutions to help leverage a competitive edge, but Xansa's experience is that this method of working has the potential to introduce additional risks and complications into a project. Some obvious challenges to success include:

- geographical separation;

- time-zone differences;

- language challenges;

- cultural differences;

- different working practices;

- barriers to building effective working relationships;

- dependence on effective supporting infrastructure;

- configuration management.

Each of these challenges can be a major issue in its own right and, if not managed effectively, may introduce potential barriers to effective communication between onshore and offshore teams. Fundamentally, the project manager cannot always see what is actually happening on the ground, and relies on effective communication at all levels to retain control. If communication fails on a project, it is easy for the project manager to lose control. And the lack of effective communication can lead to the further deterioration of working relationships, challenging the project manager's attempts to recover the situation.

Xansa has developed effective processes and working practices to manage such risks, and these are continuously improved based on actual experience. But, over time, it has become apparent that something more fundamental is needed over and above these processes to help cement the working relationship between onshore and offshore teams, and reduce the likelihood of an 'us and them' working culture emerging. With this in mind, new initiatives have been launched to introduce truly integrated onshore and offshore teams, with shared goals, managed from a single point, irrespective of location.

18.3 WHY MOVE TO THE FULLY INTEGRATED ONSHORE AND OFFSHORE MODEL?

A common observation of teams new to working with offshore delivery components is the need to go into extreme detail in specifications, certainly much more so than would be assumed necessary for their fellow UK colleagues. They code exactly as in the specification. If you don't specify error codes for read-write errors, none will be included in the programs. Indeed, some onshore project managers might argue that their analysts simply do not have sufficient technical knowledge to cover the detail required by offshore teams. However, these highly detailed specifications keep changing as the user becomes more focused on detailed requirements. The degree of detail needed and management of constant change can add up to quite an overhead on project costs, and can strain working relationships when working across remote sites.

Another common misconception is that IT workers located offshore are unable to liaise effectively with end-users or indeed fellow technicians in the UK. In reality, these should be interpreted as symptoms of an immature or ineffective working partnership, where expectations are not fully understood by either party, and communication is failing. Xansa's experience has shown that as onshore and offshore teams become fully integrated and used to working together, these issues become of manageable proportions while enabling cost saving benefits to be realized. Interestingly, where issues arise, they often tend to be a side-effect of the traditional waterfall approach to project management itself, rather than due specifically to the nature of the onshore and offshore working model.

18.4 THE BENEFITS OF COMBINING DSDM WITH THE FULLY INTEGRATED ONSHORE AND OFFSHORE RESOURCING MODEL

An obvious flaw in the waterfall approach can be its failure to anticipate that the end-user may only truly understand what is required when they see the end product that is delivered. Consequentially, scope change can be considerable, and may present significant management issues. It also depends on accurate and unambiguous specifications. These are exactly the same sort of issues that can put additional pressure on integrated offshore resourcing models. Of course, such issues are not uniquely related to this method of working, but nevertheless, they add to the list of challenges that need managing.

The DSDM approach recognizes the need to accommodate such scenarios from the outset, and projects are geared accordingly. The synergies between DSDM and fully integrated offshore delivery are now clear. Xansa has recognized that if it is possible to combine the DSDM approach with fully integrated onshore–offshore delivery teams, significant benefits can be realized, it is almost the logical next step in refining the integrated onshore and offshore delivery model itself. Conversely, without fully integrated onshore and offshore teams, implementing DSDM offsite would be a huge challenge.

Based on its experiences of fully integrated onshore and offshore delivery, Xansa has tailored the standard DSDM approach. Amendments include:

◆ addition of extra roles;

◆ modification of the suitability filter;

- addition of extra products;

- addition of extra purpose statements and quality criteria for existing products.

18.5 *TRANSITION TO DSDM OFFSITE*

Taking a long-term strategic view to DSDM offsite will help de-risk the approach, and provide an opportunity to fine-tune according to experience. A 'big bang' approach to offshore DSDM simply will not work, but the same can also be said for using the traditional waterfall approach offshore. Transition planning should be viewed within this context. The cost of managing transition should be fully considered during feasibility studies, and it may even be prudent to manage transition to DSDM offsite as a DSDM project in its own right.

Transition must be planned carefully from the outset, and the need to consider a realistic pipeline of work for the integrated team is absolutely paramount. This will allow the investment in start-up costs to be justified. If necessary, the integrated team can work on both DSDM and traditional waterfall projects in order to remain an effective working unit over a period of time.

When establishing an offsite delivery service between the UK and the offshore delivery teams, use is made of a transition stage for integrated delivery. In this stage, plans are made and executed to ensure that, for example, the necessary infrastructure, knowledge transfer and working practices are in place to allow efficient and effective DSDM working offsite. The transition phase may include temporary relocation of team members between offsite and onsite locations to assist in knowledge transfer and to ensure an accurate view of progress and issues is provided at ground level.

A staged approach to rollout between two particular delivery centers is recommended, beginning with a scenario including a 'virtual' offsite team based in the UK, delivering design and build iteration up to but not including integration testing,

Depending on the circumstances of an individual project, it may be feasible to move both functional model and design and build iterations offshore, assuming key business users are able to spend some time offshore and/or appropriate communications media are in place. A hybrid approach may also be considered during transition, wrapping elements of waterfall design and build within an overall DSDM framework.

In summary, the transition must consider:

- Is there a pipeline of work to justify investing in a truly integrated onshore and offshore team?

- Is the onshore–offshore team working as a truly integrated unit?

- What infrastructure is required to enable effective working between remote sites across different time zones?

◆ A phased approach, allowing lessons to be learned and addressed before migration to full DSDM offsite working in a risk adverse manner.

◆ Additional travel and accommodation costs that may be incurred.

18.6 AN OVERVIEW OF THE DSDM OFFSITE LIFECYCLE

Table 18.1 shows a high-level view of the DSDM process and indicates at which stages the onsite and offsite teams are most likely to be involved. In the table the following abbreviations are used.

FS = feasibility study (DSDM phase)

TRANS.PLAN. = transition planning (additional phase for offshore projects)

BS = business study (DSDM phase)

FMI = functional model iteration (DSDM phase)

DBI = design and build iteration (DSDM phase)

INT/OAT TEST = integration testing and operational acceptance testing (additional phase)

IMP = implementation (DSDM phase)

Table 18.1 Involvement of Offsite and Onsite Teams

	FS	TRANS. PLAN.	BS	FMI	DBI	INT/OAT TEST	IMP
Onsite team	Do	Do	Do	Do	Support	Do	Do
Offsite team		Offsite management involved	Developer and Technical Co-ordinator involved	Developer and Technical Co-ordinator involved working onsite	Do	Support	Support
Offsite Co-ordinator	Do	Involved	Involved				

Table continues on next page

Table 18.1 Continued

	FS	TRANS. PLAN.	BS	FMI	DBI	INT/OAT TEST	IMP
Alternative approach				FMI could take place offsite, if Ambassador User willing to relocate for FMI			

The DSDM offsite lifecycle is based around the standard DSDM lifecycle. Decisions need to be made on how the lifecycle will be used. For example:

◆ Will there be a single or multiple implementations?

◆ Will functional model iteration and the design and build iteration be run as separate or combined phases?

◆ Will DSDM be combined with elements of traditional waterfall project management techniques?

Examples of amendments to the DSDM lifecycle to accommodate offsite DSDM follow.

Feasibility Study

The feasibility study will be predominantly onsite/home based, and considers project specific details as well as the feasibility of utilizing the integrated onshore and offshore resourcing model. The feasibility study should therefore seek consultancy input from experienced practitioners of offshore working. From the outset, it is important to include input and considerations from an offsite perspective, working in partnership with onsite colleagues to ensure the approach, risks, and project details are fully understood.

Some of the additional feasibility study tasks required to facilitate DSDM offsite include:

◆ assessment of current and required infrastructure;

◆ assessment of teams' capability across both sites (technical experience, proven working relationships, DSDM knowledge);

+ de-commit criteria;

+ definition of escalation procedures;

+ definition of a high-level communication strategy;

+ potential travel costs identified and anticipated.

Business Study

Offsite involvement starts to increase from this stage onwards, and representatives of the offsite team (Project Leader, Experienced Developer) should be present during the Business Area Definition workshop. This will prove invaluable during later phases of the project. During this stage, the offsite Technical Co-ordinator will liaise with the Technical Design Authority to ensure compatibility between offsite and onsite technical platforms, and to address communication and hand-over issues.

Functional Model Iteration

Planning and workshops should be carried out onsite for the first iteration. Prototypes can be built onsite or offsite, but should be reviewed onsite. The locations for iterations two and three will have been agreed on a project-by-project basis during the business study, and could be onsite or offsite depending on suitability of each project. Particular focus must be placed on ensuring very clear objectives and acceptance criteria where offsite timeboxes are being deployed.

Design and Build Iteration

Location for the iterations can be onsite or offsite depending on a project's suitability, and may incorporate elements following the traditional waterfall approach, if prudent. However, user involvement and business testing must be planned for throughout this stage, and not left for the final iteration only. Again, any use of timeboxes offsite must incorporate very clear objectives and acceptance criteria.

Implementation

By its very nature, implementation is managed best onsite, but active involvement should be sought from the offsite Technical Co-ordinator and Experienced Developer. This can be achieved by physically moving the holders of these roles onsite, or through the use of video conferencing if more practical.

After final implementation, a combined project review should be held, to build continuous improvement into the process.

18.7 NEW DSDM ROLES TO ACCOMMODATE OFFSITE WORKING

In order to accommodate DSDM offshore working, some of the standard DSDM roles have been amended, and three new roles have been introduced: Offsite Co-ordinator, Communications Co-ordinator, and Technical Design Authority. These are roles that can be assumed by existing team members – the DSDM offsite approach is designed not to introduce additional resource overheads that might offset the cost savings of utilizing offshore in the first place.

The **Offsite Co-ordinator** is responsible for the initial approach development, ensuring that appropriate resource and commitment are gained, and shaping up the project to the point where both DSDM and Offsite are confirmed as the appropriate approaches, and an offsite project manager is appointed. This role is likely to be a leading one until the end of the business study stage. Effectively the role provides the link between offshore and onshore up to the point where the project is fully engaged.

The **Communication Co-ordinator** must take overall responsibility for communication between the onsite and offsite development centers. A full and clear focus must remain on effective communication at all levels during a project utilizing offshore resource. Failure to do so can result in minor issues being exaggerated beyond their individual importance to challenge the success of the project. Main responsibilities include the production of communication strategy in the feasibility and business studies, and an ongoing responsibility throughout the project for monitoring communication. This role is first on the escalation path for all communication-related issues.

The **Technical Design Authority** takes responsibility for the overall technical infrastructure and for compatibility between the onshore and offshore environments and technology platforms. They liaise between the Technical Co-ordinators on each site, and with the Configuration Manager.

18.8 CONCLUSIONS

As this case study shows, the need to take into account the long-term view and build fully integrated onshore–offshore working practices is paramount if cost benefits are to be fully realized. Experience gained through integrated delivery of projects and support and maintenance has proven that the commonly perceived obstacles to rolling out DSDM to onsite and offsite working are manageable. Building the capability for offsite DSDM brings a valuable extra dimension of capability to this resourcing model.

An organization considering the use of offshore resources for traditional waterfall or DSDM projects should seek advice from those who have worked in this field.

The first step in assessing potential use of offshore is to run a DSDM feasibility study. The feasibility study should seek to examine the specific issues relating to integrated onshore–offshore working, and assess the likely suitability of such an approach for your organization.

For further information on DSDM offshore, please contact Barry Fazackerley; tel. +44 (0)1244 695372.

Chapter 19

What Happens When it all Goes Horribly Wrong

Some interesting anecdotes from the experiences of Jennifer Stapleton, one of the founding members of the Consortium and editor of this book.

Obviously no matter how good a method is, it can and will go wrong if it is misapplied. A criticism often leveled at this kind of book is that it paints an unnaturally positive picture. However, life is never perfect: Murphy's Law prevails.

Each of the following stories is true; only the names have been removed, to protect the guilty. I hope they will serve as cautionary tales for the unwary.

Our Technical Co-ordinator is Missing!

Project One had a team of highly experienced developers who had worked successfully as a team for many years. Because of this, it was felt that the role of Technical Co-ordinator was unnecessary in their pilot DSDM project. They had never needed one before, why should they need one now?

As they moved from timebox to timebox, the problems mounted. No one had overall responsibility for configuration management, so it just didn't happen. Nobody was the owner of the software architecture, so the daily meetings rapidly turned from focused half-hour progress checks to lengthy discussions over what was the best approach, creating enormous delays, as no one had the ultimate say.

As a result each timebox barely scraped in with the minimum usable subset, despite working long hours as each timebox drew to a close. The products from different timeboxes did not integrate properly, causing enormous grief in the later timeboxes. The team were utterly exhausted by the end of the project, and all promptly disappeared for two weeks holiday!

The Case of the Disappearing Ambassador User

Project Two was building a financial system using a team of designers and programmers who all at some time in the past had worked on the business side. They knew it all! They constantly provided enhancements to the systems used in the area, often purely from their own analysis and ideas, which they offered to the business managers for approval and funding.

The team had always worked in the business environment, away from the IT department, and were seen to be possibly the most business-oriented group within IT. They appeared to be ideal candidates for a DSDM pilot project.

The kick-off workshop for the project went stunningly well. There did not seem to be any discord about the scope of the project, its priorities were amicably agreed and the various business roles were assigned with no concerns over commitment of time, since the whole team were all on the same floor of the building.

Issues began to arise during a business study workshop when the new business processes and roles were being defined. The developers appeared to feel that their solutions were naturally superior to those of the Ambassador User, and even those of the Visionary, the manager for the area. Despite this apparent arrogance, the Ambassador User agreed to commit three days a week to fulfilling her role in the project.

During the investigation phase of the first timebox she created the business scenario that she would use for testing. However, when she came to apply her tests in the refinement phase, she could find very few similarities between what had been agreed and what had been produced. The developers had once again assumed that they knew better. One was even heard to say, 'She doesn't understand all that we can do for her, she's too stupid!' Naturally, the Ambassador User felt her time could be used more productively elsewhere, and left the project forever.

The team continued development without her, and produced the wrong system, which failed not only on functionality, but also on usability criteria.

Timeboxes for Fun (and no Profit)

Project Three was a small project with only three developers, an 'Ambassador User', who was treated like any other customer user, and a project manager who did not understand the underlying principles of DSDM. In fact, as we will describe, he had a hazy grasp of agile programming. None of the team received any training or mentoring, and the project was run by hearsay.

The project manager produced a 'traditional' activity-based project plan, and then marked key milestones as the end of timeboxes. These 'timeboxes' had little internal structure, and were not set with the appropriate criteria. There was some prioritization but it was again more activity-based rather than being led by business requirements.

Because the 'timeboxes' were not managed in the way recommended by DSDM, many of the actual end-dates did not correspond with the original plan. When a milestone was reached (the end of a 'timebox' on the plan) and the activities were incomplete, the activities were simply extended into the next 'timebox'.

The project delivered what it was asked to, but it overran on both time and budget. The team's interest in DSDM was completely undermined, and the project management team turned their back on 'DSDM' as they could see no benefit in it.

Moral: Just calling a project DSDM, and using a few buzzwords, does not a DSDM project make.

Who Needs Testing?

Project Four was in an organization that had already adopted DSDM, to the extent of setting up a DSDM process support group. However, during the initial stages of this project, some of the key roles had been left ill-defined. For instance, no one on the development team had a clear idea of who was the Visionary for the project.

The Technical Co-ordinator's role was spread across more than one person with no specific areas of responsibility allocated to these individuals. One of the responsibilities that slipped through the net was ensuring the technical standards were followed. As a result, the developers had 'forgotten' to do anything other than simple unit testing, rather than the constant integrated testing DSDM requires. A few weeks before delivery, a testing team was added to the project to cover this shortfall and they quickly discovered a wide range of problems. It became clear that the developers had done no testing of any non-functional requirements.

Even when the specialist testing team had been brought in, there was still no prioritization of the tests carried out. The Ambassador Users and Technical Co-ordinator(s) were not consulted as to business or technical requirements. Once it was finally assembled, the product was performing very poorly and was unusable.

There was no Tester role within the teams, as this project was run under an earlier version of DSDM, but even if Testers had been present it would appear that they would not have been properly supported, because of the lack of a clear testing strategy. The Testing Strategy and Quality Plans are a fundamental part of the Development Plan, and had been neglected to the extent that the Quality Plan was still a draft document as the delivery date drew near.

We Can't Talk to the Users

Project Five was run across a split site, with the IT people and the user community being based about 50 miles apart.

Communication had initially been excellent, with workshops attended by all the necessary people and excellent decisions on priorities and scope. The project looked set fair to be a success.

Once development was under way, however, it soon became apparent that the infrastructure could not support anything more advanced than static e-mails and phone conversations. The Ambassador Users could not commit the time away from their other duties to travel to the IT department, and similarly the development team did not travel to the user site. Their reason for this was that the users' machines were incapable of supporting the development tool, making it impossible to demonstrate prototypes. The infrastructure support staff were unwilling to 'bend the rules' sufficiently to overcome this issue.

As the project progressed, the two departments became increasingly isolated, and the team spirit waned, despite the best efforts of the enthusiastic business analyst who constantly tried to bridge the gap. As this gap widened, the developers went back to talking in a 'techie' way to the users, sending highly complex, jargon-ridden documents for approval or comment. The users could not comprehend these documents, and lost interest in the project.

Despite this, the project did deliver, but the users were left with a slight feeling of resentment, as they had been looking forward to being more involved in the development process. What should have been an opportunity to bring the users' business expertise in contact with the development area instead reinforced the 'them and us' feeling.

Chapter 20

A Measured DSDM Project – BT

This chapter discusses a BT project that used Version 2 of DSDM. At the time the project was carried out BT had already used DSDM on a number of projects and it was seen as a key technique in which people should possess skills and experience. However, it was not enough for BT to use DSDM: in order to understand what DSDM would mean to the people who would be using it, it was also necessary to get a feel for the hard factors, such as time spent on different activities, and soft factors, such as the perception of the team and their levels of stress throughout the project. One major area of concern was that, although developers thoroughly enjoy working in an agile environment, they can easily burn out through intensive and prolonged working hours. The metrics collected during this project are very interesting in this area.

The case study is largely as written by Ben Whittle, the project manager. The only editing has been to remove any repetition of detail about DSDM. It would appear from the description that the team structure was not as advocated by DSDM, in that the users seem to be described as customers and were not part of the team. However, the user participation was higher than the case study suggests initially (Friday afternoons only).

20.1 THE APPROACH TO DSDM

The intention was to run the project by the book (i.e. the *DSDM Manual*) with full facilitation support, using all the key DSDM techniques in order to:

◆ get experience of DSDM;

◆ determine what worked and what didn't, and why;

◆ determine what information and experiences could be provided for others in BT and the wider community.

BT interpreted the DSDM philosophy to include:

- timeboxing;

- small team size;

- development team collocated in a 'clean room';

- working solely on one project – which is not normal practice in the unit under-taking this project;

- facilitation from DSDM experts – of which BT has a considerable body;

- no outside distractions (such as phones, other project work);

- lots of customer and user involvement, regular reviews with customers;

- restrictions of leave and training within timeboxed periods;

- use of familiar tools and techniques.

The project manager feels that it is unlikely that anyone would ever be in a situation where all of these conditions could hold true. *(Ed: This is probably because BT's interpretation is rather more restrictive than the DSDM manual which does not require clean rooms or complete lack of outside distractions.)* This is what happened on the Asset Broker project:

- Timebox: April 9, to May 24, 1996 – the timebox was created artificially with customer agreement, giving them seven weeks for a project that was estimated at 12 weeks duration (and would traditionally have taken six months as people would have been working on other projects).

- A development team of four people (with part-time scribe/manager and DSDM facilitation consultant).

- Collocation, the clean room available to the project was an open plan corral within the unit. This is probably a more realistic situation if DSDM is to become widespread – every team can't have a room to themselves.

- The development team did work virtually exclusively on the project, with the very occasional hard-fought hours for reviews of previous projects, the unit open day, and some development training courses which were not related to the project.

- Facilitation was provided by the DSDM team within BT.

- The clean room had one phone that was used as a hot-line to customers; the team members' normal numbers were diverted to the unit clerical team or answering machines. Core hours were agreed as 09:30–11:45 and 12:45–4:15

with a daily wash-up meeting at 4:15. The team answered e-mail outside core hours with only one e-mail with a project ID available to the clean room.

- The customers and users fully supported the development and nearly all visited the development at least once a week. A hot-desk was set up within the clean room so that one of the users could collocate when possible.

- Conferences and leave that had already been booked took place – in fact the original estimate of four full-time people ended up as an average of 3.2 people per day once conferences, training and leave had been taken into account. When you add the 'catch-up' time this results in a considerable drain on the project.

- The team used the NEXTSTEP OO development environment, an Oracle database and an intermediate web server for Oracle and NEXTSTEP called Webrex.

The plan was simple: take seven weeks, a week at the start for the business study, and a week at the end for implementation. This left five weeks in the middle in which they had five one-week iteration periods: three one-week functional model iterations and two one-week design and build iterations. The weekly focus meant it was easy to tell customers when to come in and review progress (Friday afternoon) and the team could go home for the weekend knowing that the customer was happy with the progress made in the week. The next week's planning could begin on Monday morning. However, once a few public holidays and open days are thrown into the cocktail, things begin to look less clear, as Section 20.3 shows.

Quality and Testing

The two key areas of concern for experienced developers when they first encounter DSDM are quality and testing. While it is not appropriate to use the most stringent quality, traceability and testing standards, the team was determined to show that the project could be engineered to a good standard. The development methods would be fit for purpose and of sufficient quality that the use of DSDM would be realistic for a development unit. The project had both electronic and paper systems, both with full indexing and configuration.

Some of the measures taken included:

- User/customer sign-off of requirements and designs, on paper copies of the requirements which were subsequently stored in the paper filing system.

- When screens were reviewed, a printout of the screen was made and any customer change requests were recorded on the printout and signed and dated by the customers. When the developer made the change, he countersigned the sheet and it was stored in the configuration file.

◆ Configuration management – use of the Devman tool – code configuration came into effect on the Monday of the second week of the functional model iteration, by the end of the project approximately 300 versions had been made, with three freezes (these freezes corresponded to ends of phases or iterations where the development had been signed off).

◆ Daily wash-up meetings, start-of-the-week planning meetings and end-of-the-week review meetings were all short and focused, with action points and decisions noted.

◆ The project team included two trained auditors, and the team invited a friendly external audit towards the end of the project to check compliance with the relevant development standards.

Since DSDM has no explicit testing phase, the project wanted to ensure that testing did not get marginalized. One of the key metrics gathered was the amount of time spent in testing and related work (see Section 20.3). Testing time and techniques on the project included reviewing screens, writing test scripts based on Use Cases and screens, code reviews, and walkthroughs. The team intended to use the CodeReviewer tool for static code analysis, but problems with installation and timescales meant that this was not possible within the timebox.

Training and Team-building

The initial intention was to train the whole team in advance of the development. However, the timebox was scheduled to begin early in a new financial year, and at short notice. As a result only the project manager went on a DSDM Practitioner course, three weeks before the project was due to start. As a result of this course, a two-afternoon (eight-hour) session was cobbled together with the facilitator, in the week before the timebox started, covering the key aspects of DSDM and serving as a project planning exercise.

No specific team-building events were scheduled, although the following events were seen as contributing to developing a team focus.

Prior to the project:

◆ During the time when the project manager was on the DSDM training course, the team was asked to specify the hardware, software, and furniture needed to kit out the clean room and assemble as much of this as possible.

◆ The two-afternoon DSDM training sessions was used to get people together to think about and agree the ways that they would work and develop and buy in to the initial project plan. Some pressure and criticism of the group on a workshop exercise was used to emphasize the benefits of team working.

During the project:

♦ The team held regular daily and weekly wash-ups, bringing everyone together to note down the achievements and difficulties of the day.

♦ The team had a regular supply of fruit, as well as the occasional doughnut which all served to bring the team together.

♦ Planning and carrying out two open days as part of the unit activity could have been seen as an overhead on the project, but planning it as a risk, being open to the visitors, and getting positive feedback, gave a valuable boost to the team.

♦ The team gave a talk to the unit half-way through the timebox. Repeating the key ideas and achievements to other people and showing what had been achieved was a great morale booster, as well as helping the relationship with the rest of the unit.

♦ On several nights (see Section 20.3), the team all agreed to work late into the evening to achieve goals.

At the end of the project:

♦ A final review was held with the customers, followed by a project review (see Section 20.5) and a meal out (where the project manager gave out small mementoes and 'survivor certificates').

♦ The team's final task together was to restore the clean room to its original condition. This activity occurred on the last day of the timebox, after delivery to the customers. Packing everything up served as a psychological closure and mourning (prior to the night out), and a means of bringing the project to a full stop and enabling another project within the unit to use the area. An end of term spirit prevailed!

The main thing to emphasize on the team-building front was the need to slaughter all the sacred cows (working practices and habits), and build a common agreement on the way of working; to regularly review this report, and to adapt to any change that would be of benefit.

Project Roles and Planning

The team consisted of four full-time people, plus one part-time (two days per week) in the project manager/customer facing role. The following roles were agreed for the project:

♦ Project Manager – external relationships, customer, and the unit.

♦ Team Leader – hour-to-hour management of progress, and working environment.

- Architect – overall system architecture, particularly database.

- Tools – e.g. configuration, code reviewer.

- User interface design.

- NEXTSTEP.

- HTML and web expert.

- Scribe – taking minutes at wash-ups, keeping documents and plans up to date.

The roles were divided across the team thus:

- Team leader and HTML expert – full-time.

- Architect and tools – full-time.

- Architect and NEXTSTEP – full-time.

- Project manager and scribe – two days per week.

- Facilitator – up to ten days over seven weeks.

External Relationships – Managing Critical Interactions

Three areas of external relationships were identified by the team and each was managed as a risk.

Customers and users

- Relationships with customers and users were managed on a daily basis.

- Organization and facilitation of more important meetings, such as the initial workshops and end of phase meetings, were done by the DSDM experts, leaving the team to concentrate on delivery.

The unit

- There was some inertia against the use of manpower in a way that was counter to the current model within the unit, and in the use of scarce developer resource on one project for an intensive period.

- Hardware and peripherals (such as the invaluable printing whiteboard) were an initial area where a great deal of time and political machination was necessary.

- The team ensured a great deal of effort went into the unit open day, and an afternoon presentation to the unit was followed up by a perception question-naire (see Section 20.3).

- There were two kinds of people who started to interrupt team progress by 'invading' the DSDM clean room: those who were generally curious and wanted to know what was going on, and those that were 'bloody-minded' and wanted to prove that they could come in (both were managed as a risk when the intrusion annoyed the team, but were not evicted as a matter of course, as this may have provoked bad feelings).

- Some team members felt a little pressure from the others in the unit making light remarks along the lines of 'being let out to play'. These were resolved by the team talking through what people felt about the remarks.

- There was an initial feeling among other people in the unit that too much pres-sure was being put on the team. The open afternoon to the unit did much to dispel these fears.

Other DSDM teams

The DSDM training course and unit open day opened the project's horizons to other teams involved in DSDM who wanted to see what they were doing and how they were get-ting along. This informal network of DSDM practitioners met together several times, and proved useful for discussing ideas and swapping hints, tips, theories, and stories.

20.2 THE PROJECT DIARY

This section records the major events in the project. The section is not intended to be a full and accurate record, but is for information purposes. The reader may like to consider the events described in this section in order to correlate events to their effects on the team. All of the dates and events are in 1996.

Date	Event
March 25–27	Project manager attends three-day DSDM Practitioner course. Team plan the clean room.
April 1–2	Short DSDM course and team project planning (two afternoons).

Project Diary table continued on next page

Project Diary Continued

Date	Event
April 9–12 Feasibility and requirements	April 9: Timebox starts: meet facilitator to agree workshop agenda, getting the clean room and tools up and running. April 11: DSDM Initiation workshop, all customers present.
April 15–19 Functional prototype 1st iteration	Goal: First cut of functional prototype screens and develop Use Cases. April 16–18: Prioritized list of customer requirements completed. Working on Use Cases with users – lots of meetings. Problems with team pressure – too many small jobs that aren't getting us anywhere. April 19: First functional prototype review (prototype) screens.
April 22–26 Functional Prototype 2nd iteration	Goal: To feed in changes to the screens and develop the functional prototype more. To get a basic Object Model from the Use Cases. April 23–25: Trying to get an Object Model from the Use Cases is getting nowhere – we try various approaches, but the effect is demotivating so we abandon it and go straight for the Object Model. Still progressing the functional prototype screens. April 26: Unit open day – much disturbance but good for morale. Second review of prototype screens goes well.
April 29 – May 3 Functional prototype 3rd iteration	Goal: To get all of the screens finished for the end of the phase, get agreement on the prioritized requirements and have a good enough Object Model to proceed with. May 1: Project presentation to the unit – increase in team morale. May 3: Second unit open day disturbance. Final day of last functional iteration. Prioritized requirements and functional prototype signed off by customers/users.
May 6–10 Design and build 1st iteration	Goal: First-cut system to show assets, demonstrating major functionality. Steady progress all week. Slower than expected. May 10: Facilitated meeting to agree a new prioritization with customers which will allow some de-scoping if progress continues at this pace. Customers happy with functionality, some small changes.
May 13–17 Design and build 2nd iteration	Goal: To have all the main functions completed. May 13–15: Major machine problems, one development machine dies, with consequent disruption to all and changes needed to configuration environment – estimated time lost: six person days. May 16: Potential problem caused by server 'feature' – decide to continue but note a possible post-implementation problem – small panic. May 17: Many late nights this week trying to

oject Diary Continued

Date	Event
	claw back from the lost days earlier in the week and the lack of support from the vendors of the server software. Goals not achieved – will have to extend into next week – more late nights. Customers happy with progress considering problems.
May 20–24 Implementation	Goal: To deliver a fully tested and partially populated system with trained users. May 24: Project delivery and customer sign-off. Initial post-project review, clean up the room, and team night out.

20.3 PROJECT DATA

Throughout the development, the team filled in a daily questionnaire. The questions were generated by the team, with the initial idea being for use by ourselves and for other people to review the project. As the project progressed, the graphs were generated and updated and were used within the team for internal management, based on an analysis of the underlying trends. The questionnaire was divided into two parts: the first dealt with the amount of time spent by the team member on different activities, the second with softer factors in the perception of the project progress. The remainder of this section will discuss the results of the study. The team filled in the questionnaire each day after the wash-up or later if they carried on working. Most of the results in the remainder of this section are averages across all of the full-time people unless otherwise stated (for example the total for the whole project includes the time spent by those who were working part-time on the project).

Effort and Resource Data

Table 20.1 contains the total project data for the development. The upper portion of the table shows the time breakdown for the four developers in the exclusive activities (individual working, etc.) with the sub-totals for working with customers and testing. DSDM places a great deal of emphasis on collocation of the team, so the team decided to measure how much time was actually spent working on their own, working together informally, at formal meetings, and the time spent on other work that was not part of the project (such as personal development, reading general e-mail, etc.). They found it very useful to measure the time spent on other work in order to monitor the total amount of effort that was being put in each day. DSDM encourages a high level of customer contact, so the project decided to measure the time spent with their customers as well. Testing is an area which has no specific phase in DSDM, so they measured testing to see what the testing profile was across the project and to see what proportion of total effort came from testing. Their definition of testing included the time spent reviewing designs and Use Cases, on code walkthrough, and module testing and developing and implementing test scripts. Lunch times were not included in the summation, but short breaks (up to ten minutes) were included.

Note that the time spent in the different types of working (individual, informal, formal, and external) is exclusive, i.e. you can only be working in one way at one time; whereas, for example, you can be informally testing with a customer, giving a value for testing, customer time, and informal meetings.

Table 20.1 *Total Time Spent on the Project*

Totals for full-time development staff	Time in hours
Individual work	502.25
Informal networking	220
Formal networking	192.25
External work	112.5
Total DSDM	914.5
Total time	1027
of which, time spent with customers	87.5
of which, time spent testing	223.75
Total DSDM team full-time	914.5
Total customer time	64.5
Facilitator time	26
Manager/scribe	118.5
Total project hours	1123.5

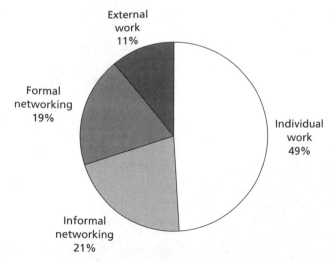

Figure 20.1 *Percentage of time in different work styles for full-time DSDM people*

Figure 20.1 shows the total time spent on the different activities for the whole project. Figure 20.2 depicts the average time spent on each task, an average of the collated results recorded by all of the engineers on the given day. Points of interest in Figure 20.2 include:

♦ a weekly cycle of iterations – effort tends to peak mid-week;

♦ individual working, informal networking and testing time increase as the project continues: formal meetings are greatest at the start;

♦ April 11: Project initialization workshop;

♦ April 16–18: Use Case workshops;

♦ April 26 and May 3: Unit open days.

The Team's Perceptions of the Project

The team considered the following questions each day, giving each a score from 1 to 6, with 1 being a disagreement with the statement and 6 being agreement. A 'don't know' (DK) response was also available.

♦ I am happy with the work in general.

♦ I feel under pressure.

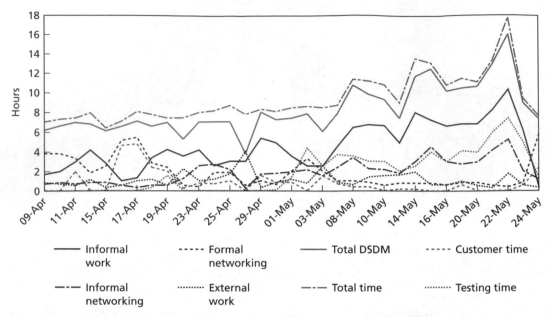

Figure 20.2 *Graph of daily effort against time for the average full-time person on the Asset Broker project*

- ◆ I feel stressed.

- ◆ I feel excessive disturbance from outside the team.

- ◆ I feel good about clean room working.

- ◆ The team is working well together.

- ◆ The development is going well.

- ◆ We will meet our requirements.

- ◆ The working environment is comfortable.

- ◆ The working environment is conducive to work.

- ◆ We're making better progress using DSDM than we would normally have done.

- ◆ The hardware (including the network) is working well.

Figures 20.3, 20.4, and 20.5 show the trends of these graphs against time. It is probably worth correlating against the project diary in the previous section, so that

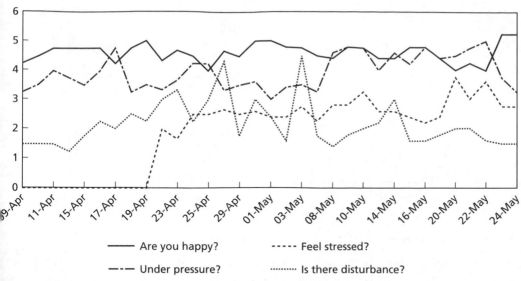

Figure 20.3 *Team perceptions of pressure and disturbance during the project,
= disagree, 6 = agree*

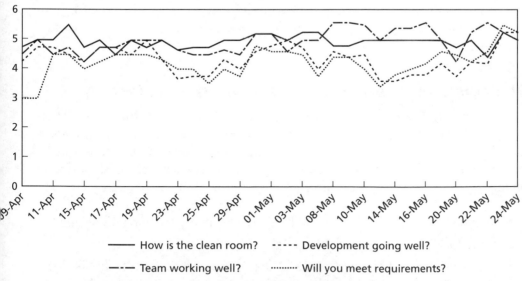

Figure 20.4 *Team perceptions of team working and progress during the project,
= disagree, 6 = agree*

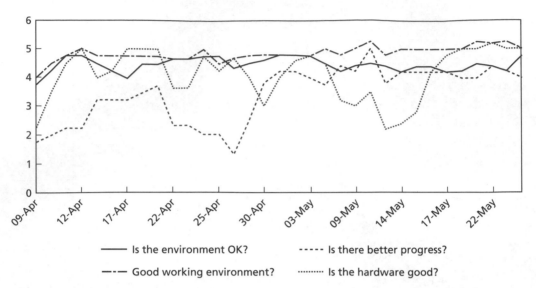

Figure 20.5 *Team perceptions of the working environment during the project, 1 = disagree, 6 = agree*

you can see the effect of events (such as the battle with Use Cases in the week ending April 26, the unit open days on April 26 and May 3, or the failure of a machine on May 13). Note that the stress question was added to the questionnaire on April 22 in order to reflect the team feeling that there was a difference between being stressed and being under pressure.

The Unit's Perception of DSDM and the Project

During the fourth week of the project, the team invited the unit to a presentation covering DSDM and the project (approximately 25 per cent of the unit members attended). In the fifth week of the project, unit members were asked to fill in a questionnaire on their perceptions of DSDM and the Asset Broker project. The meeting and the questionnaire helped the project team towards a number of goals:

◆ Helping the team to understand (and therefore manage) the relationship with the other people and projects in the unit.

◆ The team felt that the awareness of the project would help to break down people's misconceptions about the working regime and purposes.

◆ It was interesting to see what people thought about DSDM and whether they would be interested in a DSDM project, based on what they had seen of the team's work.

The questionnaire was filled in by 19 people, about 60 per cent of those who could have completed it (Table 20.2). The results were gathered from May 8–15, 1996. Questions focused on people's perceptions of RAD and DSDM, with particular emphasis on the current DSDM project. Figure 20.6 and Table 20.3 contain a more detailed breakdown of people's perceptions of the DSDM experiment (i.e. the aim of understanding more about DSDM) and of the working practices in general.

Table 20.2 *SoftLab Perceptions of DSDM (Part 1)*

Question	Yes	No
Are you aware of RAD?	19	0
Are you aware of the Dynamic Systems Development Method?	15	4
Are you aware that there is a DSDM development happening in this unit?	18	1

Table 20.3 *SoftLab Perceptions of DSDM (Detailed Breakdown) (1 = Disagree, 6 = Agree)*

	The questions	Avg	Max.	Min.	DK	Mode
Q1	Do you understand what the current DSDM experiment is aiming to achieve?	4.36	6	2	0	5
Q2	Is a DSDM experiment is the kind of thing BT should be doing?	5.36	6	5	0	5
Q3	Do you feel DSDM is a good way of working?	4.08	5	3	6	4
Q4	Would you like to be involved in a DSDM project?	4.06	6	2	2	3
Q5	Do you think the DSDM development is going well?	4.9	6	4	8	5

Table continued on next page

Table 20.3 Continued

	The questions	Avg	Max.	Min.	DK	Mode
Q6	Has the unavailability of the DSDM team caused you problems?	2.53	5	1	0	2
Q7	Do you think the DSDM team is becoming isolated?	3.86	5	2	4	4
Q8	Have you re-evaluated the way you work because of the DSDM ideas?	2.11	4	1	1	1

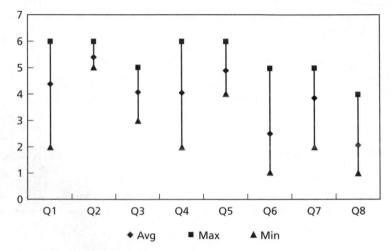

Figure 20.6 SoftLab Perceptions of DSDM (detail)

20.4 CONCLUSIONS AND LESSONS LEARNED

This case study was written to add to the current knowledge about DSDM within BT. This is a real project, some things went wrong, they had some bad luck, but they did deliver. Please don't take any of the information in this case study as literal truths for all DSDM projects. They are examples from one team on one project. Being part of a DSDM project is hard work and will not suit all people, some projects, or some units. Be prepared to adapt everything to suit the needs of the team, and play to your strengths.

The key lessons learned during the project were:

◆ Team buy-in to every decision is vital – the team must own the problems and the solutions.

- Make sure that your clean room is complete, including all installations of hardware and software tested for the way in which you intend to use them, before the timebox begins.

- Make sure up front that you know who is available when – resource is soon eroded by outside meetings, leave and courses – the team must manage this as a risk.

- Small wins – have goals for each week (or perhaps each day) so that progress can clearly be seen (draw a chart on the wall). Recognize small wins – e.g. the doughnut and cream cake bonus at the end of an iteration.

- Get customer buy-in to DSDM as well as to the project goals and keep the customers involved with the development. Manage their expectations – especially if they can't make all meetings.

- Use and build the contacts with other DSDM projects – you are not alone!

After the project had finished, a project review meeting was held at which more detailed lessons learned were identified (see Section 20.5). The main thing is that they would all work in a DSDM project again.

20.5 APPENDIX: RESULTS OF THE PROJECT REVIEW MEETING

This section records in note form the feedback on the project from the end-of-project review held on the last day of the project.

What Worked Well

Results

- system delivered in very short timebox (seven weeks): would not have been possible any other way;

- customers signed off completed system, were pleased with result and impressed by method of working.

Daily wash-ups

- brief and focused (minimum 5 minutes, maximum 30);

- effective because they were documented (decisions, actions, requirements, etc.);

- continued even when time was short and team not convinced of their usefulness.

Weekly iterations

Reviews of prototypes with customers (Friday afternoons) and team planning meetings (Monday mornings) to set goals for the week.

Clean room

A 'virtual' clean space (within open plan), worked because it was arranged well (desks in central cluster, adequate personal space, access to walls), and managed well (minimum of interruption from phones, e-mail, visitors, etc.).

Quality

- ◆ ensured by, e.g. sign-off of requirements, documented test schedules;
- ◆ helped by having auditors in team plus an invited 'friendly' audit;
- ◆ result is a quality product despite the general perception of RAD.

Process

- ◆ short timebox and 80/20 rule ensured focus on the real problem;
- ◆ external facilitation essential (in this case a DSDM support person plus an independent workshop leader);
- ◆ knowledge of the process within the team (in this case project manager was DSDM-trained);
- ◆ use of dedicated scribe invaluable, especially as she was not a developer;
- ◆ management of external interface, e.g. with rest of unit, networking with other DSDM projects;
- ◆ measurement of 'soft' metrics added to DSDM process knowledge.

People and teamwork

- ◆ team-building helped by project planning exercise combined with the DSDM overview, and by team creating the clean room;
- ◆ team all committed to success despite problems and pressures;
- ◆ good mix of personalities within team (couldn't afford any learning time);
- ◆ a Champion with drive and vision (in this case the project manager);

- core hours and other working practices agreed within the team;

- social events, mutual lunch times, supplies of food, etc., helped team spirit;

- joint working with customers, including some collocation.

What Worked Less Well – Lessons, Issues, Questions

- Planning and baselining: ensure the timebox is big enough at least to get the 'must haves' in (does RAD mean you have to work late into the night to meet the deadline?).

- As far as possible set up the environment (hardware, software, clean room) before the timebox begins.

- Testing strategy for RAD needs careful planning (e.g. what level of documentation do you need?). The team felt more support was needed from DSDM on testing.

- People work under high pressure in RAD projects – plan recuperation periods following a timebox (e.g. leave, training, wind-down, and gradual start-up, not straight into another project).

- Put risk strategies in place particularly relating to technical skills and hardware (12 days lost to hardware failure).

- Don't assume 100 per cent availability (people's time soon disappears in leave, training, open days, other projects, etc.). Actual utilization was about 60 per cent.

- Beware of customer commitment dropping off towards the end. If you are successful, they don't worry and don't think they need to attend – the inverse of what you might expect (possibly an issue of scheduling customer time up front).

For more information on this case study, contact BT Labs in Martlesham Heath, Suffolk, England.

Chapter 21

From DSDM Adhocracy to DSDM Factory

The first part of this case study shows some of the common problems that organizations encounter and the solutions that Atos Origin in the Netherlands came up with. Interestingly, the projects are a major migration, something which at first sight would be totally composed of 'must haves'. This demonstrates that it is always worth investigating what is really needed, as stated by the author, Jeroen Venneman.

The second part of this case study describes one sort of tool that can be easily produced from the DSDM manual and tailored to an organization's particular needs. Visit www.dsdm.org and download the basic tool (i.e. without any tailoring). This is for Version 3 of DSDM, which is in the public domain. Note: The DSDM Suitcase for Version 4 is only available to full members of the Consortium.

Note: The 'Adhocracy' in the title is a term coined by Jeroen to mean 'Ad hoc reaction to occurring problems'.

1.1 INTRODUCTION

After reading about principles, phases, products, techniques and the like, it may be refreshing to read how the use of all this DSDM stuff was structured during the execution of 20 projects within a project group over a period of 18 months.

This case study will focus on:

◆ The lessons learned during the (growing) use of DSDM.

◆ A 'DSDM suitcase' that was used to support the introduction and structuring of the use of DSDM.

Before addressing the 'DSDM suitcase', the project situation and the main lessons learned will be described. Finally the follow-up will be addressed.

21.2 PROJECT SITUATION

A project group was set up to migrate up to 23 applications in the period from March to December 2000. The migration can be seen as a DSDM project with a fixed end date and a fixed budget for the overall migration. Most of the individual projects, which were treated as increments, did not have a fixed end date from the business perspective. However, to control the migration project, a fixed end date was determined for each individual project. Table 21.1 shows the size and productivity, based on the first 13 applications that were delivered.

Table 21.1 *Statistics for First Applications Migrated*

Application (Powerbuilder/ Sybase)	Function point (FP)	Exclusive overhead		Inclusive overhead	
		Costs (hours)	Productivity (hours per FP)	Costs (hours)	Productivity (hours per FP)
Application 1	236	120	0.51	250	1.06
Application 2	251	149	0.59	287	1.14
Application 3	137	132	0.96	207	1.51
Application 4	139	150	1.08	226	1.63
Application 5	1344	1906	1.42	2645	1.97
Application 6	145	271	1.87	351	2.42
Application 7	130	299	2.30	371	2.85
Application 8	224	569	2.54	692	3.09
Application 9	336	900	2.68	1085	3.23
Application 10	578	1768	3.06	2086	3.61

ble 21.1 *Continued*

Application (Powerbuilder/ Sybase)	Function point (FP)	Exclusive overhead		Inclusive overhead	
		Costs (hours)	Productivity (hours per FP)	Costs (hours)	Productivity (hours per FP)
Application 11	228	888	3.89	1013	4.44
Application 12	176	959	5.45	1056	6.00
Application 13	215	1344	6.25	1462	6.80
Total	**4139**	**9455**	**2.28**	**11731**	**2.83**

Size and productivity based on the first 13 applications that were delivered (overhead is estimated on 0.55 hour per function point).

Lessons Learned about a Fixed End Date

If there is not enough pain on the business side when running beyond the overall time-box for the increment, difficulties with prioritizing can easily arise during workshops.

This risk was addressed by focusing on

♦ The fixed end date (additional wishes can be placed on the 'parking spot' and become part of another project). Note: The 'parking spot' is a sheet of brown paper that is used during workshops to park items (on Post-Its) that must be addressed at a later time.

♦ The scope, i.e. limiting it to the migration.

♦ Fitness for business purpose.

♦ Making use of an independent facilitator with DSDM knowledge.

When talking about a migration project, many people expect a fixed functionality project. Therefore it needs to be emphasized that in this case the original application is not migrated one to one. Only the high-level functionality from the processes relating to the original application was taken as a starting point. The details would come forward during later workshops.

Additional challenges came from the fact that many of the applications changed from local to nation-wide applications, some of the applications would be integrated into one new application, and a technical maintenance department for the different applications had to be set up during development.

Lessons Learned about the Kick-off Meeting

The kick-off meeting with representatives of all stakeholders is very important. It was used:

- to identify missing stakeholders by visualizing the stakeholders on a sheet of brown paper;
- to make clear why the development is taking place;
- to define the scope;
- to confirm the empowerment within the scope;
- to explain DSDM and its impact;
- to emphasize that it would not be a one-to-one migration, but that we would rebuild and redesign the current application by working from the global process to more details in a later phase.

Lessons Learned about the Involvement of Functional and Technical Maintenance Departments

These departments must be involved during development to facilitate the acceptance of the system.

- If the technical maintenance department was set up during development, they could be involved during the design and build iteration and support the test and review.
- The functional maintenance department played a key role in the selection of the right representatives, the communication to the wider user group, and the implementation plan (including training users).

DSDM was chosen as the development method, but where did this choice come from and was there any support from the organization?

In spite of some earlier successes with DSDM in the organization, DSDM was not embedded organization-wide, and there was no support for setting up a DSDM project. For the project group, the choice was mainly triggered by individual contacts between the project manager and people involved in the earlier successes. These individual contacts finally resulted in the necessary approval of the customer organization and the account team.

Since there was no support available from the organization, the only support in the use of DSDM came from two DSDM practitioners who participated in the first team.

During the first project, a structure to capture the requirements as well as the communication surrounding the test had to be defined.

Lesson Learned about Testing

Testing needs special attention.

A test manager role is very important, because it optimizes the communication between IT and business. Points of attention for the test manager are:

- ◆ Investigate the dependencies in the user environment, the test experience of the users and the total number of users/locations/departments.

- ◆ Emphasize that everything must be tested.

- ◆ Structure the test to support the end users with the execution, be able to monitor progress, and deliver a test-set based on the requirements for the technical maintenance department.

- ◆ Guide the creation of the user manual by the end users as part of structuring the test.

Many developers love to start refining the prototype before updating the requirements. Since the requirements must be the prime focus, it is important that defining or updating requirements is easy.

The two certified DSDM practitioners had already worked on a requirement registration tool, and this tool was worked out in more detail within the project group. The tool can be used to register requirements in a database. The requirements are presented in a tree view: the project at level one, high-level requirements at level two, and the details at the following levels.

Test cases can be added to requirements, and different overviews can be printed to support the way of working.

The technical test by the developers needs special attention. A procedure was defined for review by a peer developer. A checklist supports this review. Tested aspects are technical, but also include the completeness of the solution, comments in code and the definition of possible test cases.

Lessons Learned about Configuration Management

The configuration management role is very important, especially when maintenance of a delivered system becomes involved, and during testing. Since the system is growing very fast towards the result, it may be needed to keep a particular situation stable for some time to carry out some test cases. Next to this, it is important to know which problems are fixed in a particular version.

It must be possible to restore a particular (known) frozen situation. This situation includes code as well as requirements.

While the first application was developed, a second team was set up. This way the number of teams grew to five. With the growing number of teams and the necessity to improve the project structure to support maintenance, it was recognized that 'ad hoc' problem solving no longer sufficed.

Lessons Learned about IT Roles Within the Development Team

There are different roles (like developer and scribe) that need to be clearly divided between the involved people. It is important to be clear about the different roles that people have and that the responsibilities related to the roles are known. This is especially important when teams become large, or when there are changes in the composition of teams.

In order to restructure the organization within the project group to accommodate an optimal use of DSDM, the 'DSDM suitcase' was developed.

Lesson Learned about Tool Support

Perhaps the most important lesson learned is this: You can improve and support the development process by making use of tools, but the quality of the team is even more important. A fool with a tool is still a fool.

21.3 THE 'DSDM SUITCASE'

What is the 'DSDM Suitcase'?

It is a PowerPoint presentation that serves as a portal to a number of templates and checklists. These templates and checklists are organized by the DSDM process model. Additional information concerns organization-specific and DSDM-specific documentation.

The 'DSDM suitcase' is based on DSDM Version 3 and its purpose is to create a project structure that is repeatable, flexible, and supports a learning organization.

How is the Information in the 'DSDM Suitcase' Structured?

It starts with a picture of the DSDM process model (see Figure 21.1) with buttons that lead to additional DSDM information: 'DSDM Principles', 'DSDM critical success factors', 'Benefits of DSDM', 'Test stages', 'Techniques', and 'Roles'.

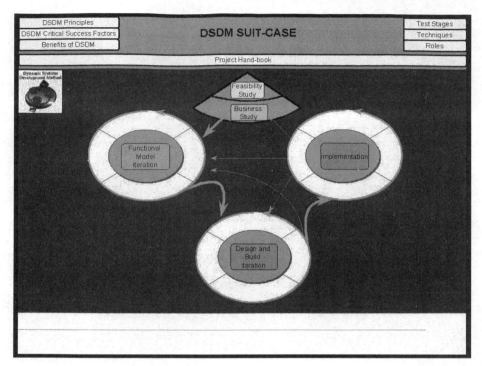

Figure 21.1 *Top level of 'DSDM suitcase'*

Another button leads to additional organization-specific information:

◆ Suitability/Risk List;

◆ links to other DSDM products (like a list of risks);

◆ template for workshop reports;

◆ list of standards and work instructions;

◆ list of procedures;

◆ list of items for the project evaluation;

◆ template for the project evaluation;

◆ templates related to maintenance (registration of problems/wishes);

◆ templates related to request forms, installation guide, user guide, requirement and test documentation, documentation generated from comment in code.

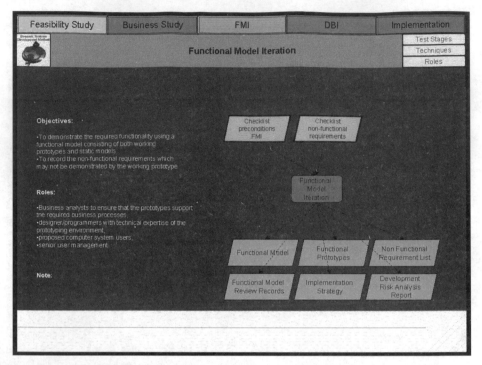

Figure 21.2 Example of a phase view

By clicking on a phase at the top level, the details of a phase come forward, as shown in Figure 21.2. These details include a visualization of the phase, the related DSDM products, and a checklist with preconditions for that phase. Beside this picture, information is given concerning the objectives of the phase and the DSDM roles involved.

By clicking on a further checklist in the visualization, a checklist is presented with a button that can be used to add a link to an organization-specific checklist.

By clicking on a DSDM product, the details of that product come forward, as in Figure 21.3. These details include information related to the purpose of the product, quality criteria, and the suggested accepters. By clicking on the button next to the product, a word document is opened containing an organization-specific template for the product.

The quality criteria are captured in a checklist that can be reached via the checklist button.

All organization-specific checklists and templates are organized in a predefined directory structure and can be reached via buttons in the presentation.

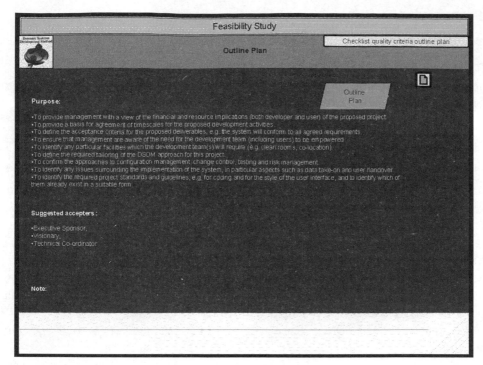

Figure 21.3 *Example of a DSDM product view*

How is the 'DSDM Suitcase' Used?

At the start of a project the 'DSDM suitcase' is installed, and a copy of the presentation and the underlying directory structure with the checklists and templates is downloaded. Now that the basic project structure is defined, the 'DSDM suitcase' can be filled, adjusted, and enhanced for the specific situation (flexible).

The development process is supported by the information presented at the different levels in the 'DSDM suitcase'. The preconditions and purposes of the phases guide the development process, and the templates for the products and their quality criteria support their production and structure the information that needs to be addressed.

A project-specific filling, adjustment, or enhancement can be suggested for integration in the 'DSDM suitcase'. This leads to the fact that if you want to be supportive to a learning organization, maintenance on the 'DSDM suitcase' is needed, and changes need to be managed by version control.

21.4 FOLLOW-UP

Project Group

Because of its successes, the project group did not end with the migration of the 23 applications. At the time of writing (2001), the project group is still receiving assignments and there are plans to integrate it in the organization.

'DSDM Suitcase'

The 'DSDM suitcase' has been taken as a starting point for the development of an organization-wide DSDM development model. This organization-wide model must incorporate different (architecture) standards in a usable form, and is being developed by another department within the organization.

The 'DSDM suitcase' turned out to be very useful as a communication means to introduce DSDM into the organization. The use of DSDM as a 'hat-rack' for the project structure and the incorporation of architecture standards, the possibilities for a learning organization (knowledge management), and its clear usability are examples of items that were discussed during demonstrations.

The basis of the 'DSDM suitcase' will be available to members of the DSDM consortium.

For more information on this case study, contact Jeroen Venneman, Atos Origin, the Netherlands. Tel: +31 (0) 6 51258756. E-mail: Jeroen.Venneman@atosorigin.com.

Chapter 22

DSDM in Process Improvement

This chapter is an abridged version of a report to the European Systems and Software Initiative (ESSI), a pan-European initiative to identify methods for process improvement and to disseminate the results across the European Community. Part-funding is available from ESSI for Process Improvement Experiments (PIEs), each of which must provide quantitative data on the process area being investigated.

This particular PIE was conducted by a Swedish part of SchlumbergerSema, with particular focus on project management and the quality of products. The author, Thomas Kalita of SchlumbergerSema InfoData, defines the metrics and methods of measurement and provides the results that show how DSDM helped SchlumbergerSema InfoData improve in these areas.

22.1 BACKGROUND INFORMATION

SchlumbergerSema InfoData, with 400 employees, is a subsidiary of SchlumbergerSema, a leading information technology services company, with 30,000 employees. InfoData's business has three main strands. First, there is InfoTorg (literally 'information market'), an online service providing fast, direct access to hundreds of Scandinavian and international databases. Second, there is a major business in direct marketing. And finally there is the most recent business area, InfoCom, which includes e-commerce, call-center and business outsourcing services.

SchlumbergerSema InfoData, like many other development organizations, has seen increasing demands from customers for faster product deliveries while at the same time it has experienced large variances in project results. This has led SchlumbergerSema InfoData to examine its current development methods, identify weaknesses within the development processes being used, and to investigate alternative new development approaches.

For the experiment, SchlumbergerSema InfoData has identified DSDM as a development approach that promises to provide improvements compared to older methods. It has the support of many prestigious UK companies, but has not been widely used in other European countries.

Within the DSDM2L2 experiment, SchlumbergerSema InfoData has used as the baseline project (the business case which DSDM is applied to in the experiment) a major product development on InfoTorg's internet portal (www.infotorg.sema.se). The main goal of the baseline project was to create a new service for InfoTorg's internet customers (business-to-business), namely a new way of accessing information on the InfoTorg internet portal.

The goals SchlumbergerSema InfoData seeks to achieve will improve the development processes and have a direct impact on SchlumbergerSema InfoData's business. SchlumbergerSema InfoData expects to have better managed projects and deliver higher quality products with improved delivery performance. The results presented in this report are supported by business and development metrics to track the results and to establish the benefits of the DSDM framework.

Experiment Objectives and Means of Measurement

Objective: Improve on-time delivery and customer satisfaction (20%).
Method: On-time delivery was assessed through measurement of the baseline's real delivery date against the planned deadline compared to the real and planned deadlines of similar SchlumbergerSema InfoData projects started and completed during the last two years (four projects).

Customer satisfaction was measured in two ways:

1. Experiment project's adherence to planned resources (person hours) compared with an average of similar SchlumbergerSema InfoData project's adherence to planned resources (the four projects mentioned above). Of course the on-time delivery aspect can also be seen as a measurement of internal customer satisfaction.

2. In the external customer satisfaction measurements, we collected data from our sales systems. We measured the baseline's revenues under the first three months and compared them to the resources spent in the project (person hours). This ratio was compared to a similar project's (regarding marketing activities) ratio. In this way we measured the baseline project's effect on SchlumbergerSema InfoData's results (Income Statement) and, indirectly, external customer satisfaction.

Objective: Increase process predictability; higher maturity level (10%).

Method: To measure the experiment project's effect on the process maturity we measured the baseline against the CMM (Capability Maturity Model; a reference model which describes and judges systems development processes). We also measured a reference project against CMM and compared the baseline against the reference project. The measurements were performed with external assistance (Q-Labs).

Objective: Improve organizational skills of both management and development personnel (20%).

Method: We used a questionnaire to measure this objective. The questionnaire was created with people working with process improvements and measurements in system development projects. The questionnaire covers areas such as Project Management (planning, monitoring, follow-up, project organization, administration, training, problem, and change management), Team Management, Quality, Collaboration and Co-operation, and Roles. The comparison was made against the same project as was used in the CMM comparison.

22.2 STARTING SCENARIO

Experiment Context

SchlumbergerSema InfoData has partly been formed by mergers and acquisitions. This has led to the situation within SchlumbergerSema InfoData today where there are different system development processes practiced. We need to be more uniform and develop the following areas:

- project planning;
- project tracking and oversight;
- software quality assurance;
- software configuration management;
- release management;
- requirements management.

The process improvement activities aim at giving SchlumbergerSema InfoData a standardized development framework that will:

- highlight task overruns in time;
- highlight project overruns in time;

- give the developers an understanding of their objectives in the context of overall project objectives;

- transfer skills between employees.

In order to continuously improve SchlumbergerSema InfoData's system development framework and address future opportunities, SchlumbergerSema InfoData needs to further improve its skills in the project management process and focus on:

- Well-defined project management practices. Excellent skills are required for setting up projects and understanding the different roles and skills needed for a development team.

- Well-defined project tracking and control methods.

- Well-defined requirements methods.

- Continual involvement of the business people and users in the project.

- Well-defined scheduling and estimation techniques.

Company Context

SchlumbergerSema InfoData, a relatively flat organization, sells information and e-services to develop the business and activities of companies and organizations. The main motivation for SchlumbergerSema InfoData in establishing the PIE, strongly supported by top management, is to improve its performance towards customers and to establish such improvements on a permanent and lasting basis throughout the organization.

The DSDM approach is well suited for replication. The experiment and in particular the extra metrics will provide the supporting data to gain acceptance of DSDM throughout SchlumbergerSema InfoData and to replicate its use throughout the organization.

Baseline Project Context

InfoTorg (short for information market) is the leading Swedish online service as well as the foremost Swedish gateway service. Operated by SchlumbergerSema InfoData it provides access to two-thirds of the public databases online in Sweden and hundreds of foreign databases.

InfoTorg has gateways to about twenty-five Swedish and some foreign online services. The contents include about a hundred Swedish databases ranging from official and legal to business information. The foreign databases cover virtually all areas.

Examples of databases accessible via InfoTorg are:

- the official company register of Sweden (PRV);
- Swedish and European patent databases;
- the official automobile register of Sweden;
- the Swedish telephone directory online;
- the postal zip codes directory.

Today information is divided into separated services, and users subscribe to one or more services on InfoTorg. The user can only search and retrieve information in a service he or she subscribes to. A goal for InfoTorg is to integrate information from these services. If a user has found information in one service, e.g. a company in the official company register, it is sometimes possible to navigate to another service with company information and automatically transfer search keys from the first service to the next. In the future, we see a need to become more user- and information-focused and less database-centric.

In the business plan for InfoTorg, there has been a manifestation of will to focus on the information itself instead of the different services. The customer should not be forced to find out where to find a certain piece of information.

In the new system built for the internet, namely the baseline project named InfoTorg MIX, information has been compiled independently of how it happens to be spread around in different services and databases. The users access the information by means of a web browser (HTML).

The objective was to integrate pieces of information stored in separate databases by using a 'multi-search function'. Instead of searching in each database, the user should be able to receive the requested data in only one 'search'. The information was to be presented on the same web page. The result of the project became a product, and a new service too, called InfoTorg MIX. InfoTorg MIX was given three basic functions:

- a search possibility for identifying private citizens, companies, and organizations;
- a few, specified, data for verification of a chosen private citizen, company, or organization;
- information packages providing information for contact use (managed by the multi-search function).

The data in the information packages was collected from existing database services.

The multi-search function mentioned above and its requirements were the main reasons why a technical change became even more interesting than it already was at the time. A decision was made that a new technical architecture should be implemented. Basically, the new architecture involved a superserver in the mainframe, which reused exisiting information servers. In the web environment new Java architecture (using Java server pages, servlets, and beans) was implemented in order to create a more dynamic environment to work in, resulting in a more flexible treatment and presentation of the data being used. The presentation layer (JSP) can easily be rewritten to suit other presentation media, for example WAP or voice. Also, the new architecture simplified maintenance and the addition of new information and provided a high grade of reusability.

The baseline project started in January 2000 and ended May 2000. Six people were involved on a full-time basis, a common project size in SchlumbergerSema InfoData. The team members spent some time on experiment activities, although most of the preparation work on the experiment was performed during fall 1999. It was a stable team, i.e. no people were incoming or outgoing, in adherence to the DSDM approach.

The development tools and languages used in the project were COBOL, DB2, TSO, Magic Draw (UML-Tool), Visio 2000 (for some diagrams), Visual Age for Java (JAVA, JDBC and Configuration Management) and Websphere Studio (JSP, HTML).

Today InfoTorg MIX is used by an increasing number of customers.

22.3 EXPERIMENT DESCRIPTION

Overview

The DSDM2L2 experiment has focused on adopting the DSDM principles for project management within the baseline project. These principles are focused primarily at:

- project leadership;
- project organization;
- roles to play within the project;
- skills and responsibilities of roles;
- teamwork;
- incremental delivery (project planning);
- iterative development cycles (project planning);
- project–customer relationships.

These principles and practical advice on how to apply them are what is provided by the DSDM framework. Applying these principles has meant quite a few changes in project practices and processes compared to what SchlumbergerSema InfoData uses today:

Active user involvement

Users on all levels are closely involved in the project from start to finish. They are not only asked to participate now and then, they are actually part of the project team on an equal footing with the developers. Three of the seven to eight roles defined within DSDM for a project team are user roles. Two Product Managers were, in the baseline, given Ambassador User roles, the most active DSDM user role in the daily project work. Normally the SchlumbergerSema InfoData Product Managers are more loosely involved in the system development process, but in this project two were the team members, participating very actively in the whole development lifecycle. This was a success, since all the project members in one of the questionnaires answered that they want the product managers to be team members in future projects.

It is not easy to find representative Ambassador Users when you develop for the internet, since it is hard to define who the users are and getting access to them. Still, this is one of our most common development situations. Does this mean that we have not used DSDM fully? I am convinced that this is not the case, since in the baseline the Ambassador Users, in adherence to the DSDM philosophy, have:

- Kept track of the customers' needs and wants (e.g. we made an early presentation of the product at a external customer seminar and used the feedback in later development work).

- Provided key input to business requirements and design sessions.

- Provided the detail of business scenarios.

- Communicated with other user representatives (Advisor Users).

- Provided input into prototyping sessions.

- Revised documentation.

- Revised and accepted timeboxes.

- Provided user documentation (product leaflets).

- Trained sales personnel and customer service personnel.

- Organized and controlled user testing.

- Been part of the steering committee to stress the importance of the role.

Collocated project team

Several of the nine principles within DSDM require good teamwork in order to be successful. Developers, users, and management must have a co-operative attitude. Decisions and contacts must be made swiftly. This means that collocation of project members is almost a tenth principle. The project team was collocated; both developers and users (business people), automatically decreasing the 'cultural gap' that can be apparent in software development between business people and developers. This has really been an important success factor. In addition the steering committee will require, where possible, all the future SchlumbergerSema InfoData projects to collocate business and development staff.

Incremental delivery

Delivering business benefits quickly and frequently is one of the basic DSDM principles. Functionality is delivered piece by piece, beginning with the most valuable business functions. In the project, we delivered incrementally, enjoying all the benefits of getting feedback early.

Project planning

DSDM requires a project to set a time at which certain business functionality is to be finished. The time target is always adhered to. If there are any problems or unforeseen circumstances, the business functions with the lowest priority are moved out of the target functionality. This way of thinking makes sure that the project is delivered on time. This business and time focus of planning is a different mindset from practices where focus is on having a piece of software finished according to the specification. We actually planned and delivered three timeboxes according to the planned overall timebox (planned at the end of the business study) with no need for overtime work. The focus was not on delivering systems or software according to specification, but on delivering business functionality fit for its purpose. The project has been a success according to adherence to budget (mainly person hours) and deadlines, at the same time delivering almost 100 per cent of the planned, changed and added functionality (remember DSDM uses an evolutionary approach).

Project management

Project management was done with a clear role-based organization. Developers focused on delivering business benefit rather than matching specifications. Developers constantly worked with the Ambassador Users, rather than consulting them now and then. The project manager worked through setting objectives instead of defining activities.

Phases of the Experiment

Work package: DSDM training

In order to embark on a DSDM project, all involved staff need sufficient training. The planned courses are as follows:

- one-day DSDM awareness training;
- three-day DSDM practitioner training;
- two-day DSDM management training;
- three-day team-building and soft skills training;
- preparation for team-building and soft skills training aligned with experiment and actual project.

Comment

This work package is regarded as completed, although two deliverables have not been delivered, namely the DSDM management training and team-building courses. The reasons are:

- During the experiment the project manager has certified himself as a DSDM Practitioner, DSDM Trainer and DSDM Examiner so most of the DSDM management training has been on-the-job training with the team. This was done for cost reasons and because we believe that this is more valuable.

- Most of the team members have worked together before, so we only needed some internal team-building activities.

Work package: Quality

In order to make sure the project applied DSDM principles stringently and correctly from the start, SchlumbergerSema InfoData needed to establish DSDM quality assurance. This means using a mentor with DSDM experience, probably from the UK. It also means having a DSDM quality assurance role on the project team who ensures on a day-to-day basis that the project adheres to the DSDM approach. The approach is to have a mentor for support if needed, but to have most of the effort of checking adherence to the framework performed by SchlumbergerSema InfoData personnel.

Activities within this work package include the following:

- advice and guidance from DSDM mentor;

- additional quality assurance activities to support DSDM;

- definition of DSDM in the context of SchlumbergerSema InfoData's technical architecture.

Comment

We did not use an external DSDM mentor, since we found an internal DSDM mentor stationed in Sundsvall (north Sweden).

To secure the quality of the DSDM2L2 still further the project manager has, as mentioned, used some of his time becoming an accredited DSDM practitioner, DSDM Trainer, and DSDM Examiner.

Work package: Applying DSDM

Within this work package are all of the activities required to implement DSDM for the baseline project. The DSDM approach involves several new activities in preparation for development, as well as actions and procedures for managing the ongoing development project. For a proper DSDM project, a feasibility and business study must be done in a defined manner. A structured DSDM business study is needed.

Activities within this work package include the following:

- understanding DSDM business study products;

- DSDM business study;

- developing the additional study information required for DSDM;

- applying DSDM principles and procedures to the baseline project.

Comment

The deliverables in this working package have taken longer than planned. It was harder than expected to do the proper DSDM feasibility and business studies and create reusable template documents.

Work package: Measurement

The objective of the experiment is to find out whether the application of DSDM principles improves development processes as well as teamwork and customer satisfaction. In order to do this, SchlumbergerSema InfoData needs to first establish a set of metrics to measure improvements in the areas of most interest. Within the project three types of tools will be used to measure the improvements related to applying DSDM:

- Process metrics to determine the overall performance of the development team.

- Organizational metrics to determine the team's ability to work together and to co-ordinate activities.

- Customer satisfaction metrics to determine the degree to which the project performance meets and exceeds customer expectations.

Activities within this work package include the following:

- Selection of project performance metrics for monitoring experiment improvements.

- Performance measurements of the experiment development project and other projects.

- Collection of process metrics throughout experiment.

- Adapting survey tools for measuring organizational effectiveness.

- Conducting organizational surveys at the start, middle, and completion of the experiment.

- Adapting survey tools for measuring customer satisfaction.

- Conducting customer satisfaction surveys at the start and completion of the experiment.

Comment

Q-labs, as mentioned, helped us with measurement and comparison to a similar project outside the experiment project and CMM. The rest of the measurements and surveys were done by ourselves, using historical and new data. Since the 'new' baseline project was selected to represent the everyday business of SchlumbergerSema InfoData, the way to measure the result needed to change slightly. The original baseline project was a traditional client development. The new project was a service development on an internet portal, making it harder to measure the business impact since it is based on selling transactions, not performing consulting hours close to the customer. Nevertheless, it has at least the same importance as the methods selected.

Work packages: Dissemination and project management

Sema Group will participate in both national and international dissemination events to discuss its experiences, both positive and negative, in adopting the elements of the DSDM framework. Activities within this work package include the following:

- ◆ Participation in two separate Swedish events focused on disseminating the results and experiences of the DSDM2L2 experiment.

- ◆ Participation in two international events organized through ESSI activities where SchlumbergerSema InfoData will present their experiences.

- ◆ Co-operation with ESPINODEs and other ESSI projects.

SchlumbergerSema InfoData will establish an Experiment Manager for the experiment to ensure projects schedules are met, to co-ordinate activities, and to address any issues that might arise. The Experiment Manager will provide the required project reports and cost statements to the Commission.

Comment

The first and second national disseminations have been performed and appreciated by the audience. A problem is that we have not yet identified the international dissemination activities.

22.4 RESULTING SCENARIO

Technical Impact

Table 22.1 shows the quantitative results obtained from the experiment.

Table 22.1 *Quantitative Results*

Objectives	Measurement	Results	Comments
Improve on-time delivery and customer satisfaction (20%)	Average SchlumbergerSema InfoData project adherence to the delivery deadline/ baseline adherence to the delivery deadline.	Compared with the average SchlumbergerSema InfoData project, the baseline was 20% better regarding on-time delivery.	Baseline result not included in the average.

Table continued on next page

Table 22.1 *Continued*

Objectives	Measurement	Results	Comments
Improve customer satisfaction (20%)	Average SchlumbergerSema InfoData project adherence to planned resources/baseline adherence to planned resources.	Compared with the average SchlumbergerSema InfoData project, the baseline was 26.1% better regarding resource planning.	Baseline result not included in the average.
Improve customer satisfaction (20%)	Baseline project resources person hours spent against revenues obtained in the first three months compared with the reference project ratio.	Regarding revenues and resources spent, customers were 22.2% more willing to buy the results of the baseline than the compared project. This could be an indicator that they are more satisfied with the baseline's deliverables.	Here we had trouble finding more than one relevant reference project, which makes the results uncertain.
Increase process predictability; higher maturity level (10%)	The baseline and the reference project were measured against the CMM and Key Process Areas: Requirements Management, Project Planning, Project Tracking & Oversight, Software Quality Assurance, and Software Configuration Management.	Quote from the Q-Labs report: 'It is clear that the implementation has increased the process maturity as related to the CMM by 40% ± 20%. The effect of using DSDM was particularly evident in the areas of Requirements management, Project planning and Project tracking and oversight. Judging by the results, DSDM seems to be a method that is particularly suited for the type and size of projects that were evaluated.'	

Table continued on next page

Table 22.1 Continued

Objectives	Measurement	Results	Comments
Improve organizational skills of both management and development personnel (20%)	A questionnaire was used to compare the baseline against a reference project.	Analysis of the answers showed that the baseline got 79% better scoring compared with the	All full-time system developers from each project answered the questionnaire (four from reference project. each project). The total questions that could be answered were 280 and we got 268 answers, which means that 4.3% of questions were not answered. The questionnaire has a structure that makes it possible for use in evaluations of future projects and it can thereby serve as a cornerstone for continuous future process improvements decisions.

Business Impact

One of the most interesting measures in our experiment project is the impact of the baseline (and indirectly the experiment) on the income statement (one of our customer satisfaction measures above). More derived results are:

◆ The adherence to deadlines with the help of the DSDM framework in the baseline has shown that we will be able to prepare market activities earlier in the future, since we are sure that the developed product will be able to be launched on the planned date. In addition, time to market naturally increases, since we will be able to sell a product with business value (80/20 rule) earlier.

◆ We have used an 'open' method, complemented with the documentation that has been created for the experiment, to improve our system development processes. Thanks to this we will be able to replicate the results, i.e. the benefits are built into the 'walls' of the organization instead of into the heads of SchlumbergerSema InfoData's people.

Organization Impact

All senior managers in the steering committee have said, based on the results of the experiment, that DSDM should be used in future projects whenever possible. This means that:

- The Product Managers will participate in the development process on a team member basis and actively collect end-users' comments.

- The business and development staff will be collocated.

- The development process will be incrementally based, instead of waterfall based, meaning that the marketing activities must also be delivered incrementally.

- Timeboxing, workshops, prototyping and functionality prioritizing will be used in adherence to the DSDM approach.

- The focus in project management will be on delivering business benefit on time rather than matching specifications. Project managers will be focused more on objectives than on defining activities.

Culture Impact

Top management support and involvement have made a strong impact on the importance of the experiment in the organization. At the same time it is recognized that a part of the baseline success measured might have relied on senior management involvement. On the other hand, the problem identification and the measurement provide senior management with the 'hard facts' that the organization must constantly try to improve its development processes since they have a real effect on the bottom line.

The collocation of the team has made it easy to communicate the PIE objectives. Furthermore, the feedback from the work on the different work packages was directly forwarded both from project management to team members and from team members to project management. This, together with senior management involvement, has probably increased motivation for the PIE.

The collocation of the project team, both developers and users (business people), has really been an important success factor, automatically decreasing the cultural gap that can be apparent in software development between business people and developers.

Skills Impact

Participants in the DSDM2L2 have increased their knowledge in the following ways:

◆ The DSDM training has improved DSDM skills in the organization.

◆ The collocation of the team has given business and development people a common language with which to communicate with each other. Incremental delivery, iterative delivery, and prototyping used in DSDM and the experiment have been supporting elements to the reduction of the semantic gap between developers and users.

22.5 KEY LESSONS LEARNED

Technological Point of View

1. DSDM is a framework that promises adherence to deadlines, a system fit for business purpose, no budget overruns, and inherent quality. The measurements in the experiment really support these statements.

2. A collocated team, both developers and users taking part actively in the development cycle, leads to a more effective and efficient project.

3. Top management support is a success factor for process improvements.

Business Point of View

4. System development process improvements must be accompanied by organizational improvements (for example new roles for the product managers created a need for flexibility regarding the movement of product managers between different projects) and changes in the business processes (for example, incremental delivery created a need for incremental marketing activities).

5. Process improvements take a lot of time and energy from an organization. They should be managed as a project with clear objectives and measurements according to plan. Perhaps the DSDM philosophy, starting with the most important first and keeping deadlines, could be a success factor for process improvements projects.

22.6 CONCLUSIONS

Objectives	Conclusions
Improve on-time delivery and customer satisfaction (20%)	The actual improvement was 23% (average)
Increase process predictability; higher maturity level (10%)	The actual improvement was 40%
Improve organizational skills of both management and development personnel (20%)	The actual improvement was 79%

For further information, contact Thomas Kalita at thomas.kalita@infodata.sema.se.

Chapter 23

DSDM and Business Rules

In this case study, Rob van Haarst demonstrates how a rigorous business rules method fits in to the DSDM framework. He outlines the method and uses a specific project to show how it is complementary to DSDM. At each phase he shows how the business rules are integrated with the DSDM products.

Note: USoft is the name of a rules engine which has been widely used in DSDM projects. At the time this case study was written, it was also the name of the company. Since then they have changed their company name (but not the product name) to NESS Technologies.

23.1 INTRODUCTION

Between August 2000 and January 2001, a functional prototype was delivered to a large European local government organization who wanted to modernize the way they were giving support to small businesses and starter businesses. This project was explicitly conducted according to both DSDM and business rules based methodology (BRM) by USoft, the business rules technology vendor.

The aim of this case study is to show how DSDM and BRM can benefit from each other, using the business case as an illustration, and to explain why they have a natural affinity.

The aim of the project itself, codenamed ACUMEN, was different. The project had, in fact, two aims:

◆ To deliver a software application to help the customer organization do its job more efficiently, and in particular to be more responsive to continual changes in laws and regulations.

◆ Generally to evaluate the suitability of DSDM and BRM for similar future projects within that organization.

The second aim was covered by several reports, including an interim report at the end of the functional model iteration phase, and by sessions between USoft and customer representatives.

How this Chapter is Organized

To create a frame of reference, we will first give an informal description of the project.

DSDM principles will not be reiterated here, but Section 23.3 offers a quick tour of business rules methodology and technology for those unfamiliar with it. Section 23.4 is a discussion of how BRM shaped activities during the three project phases. The last section (23.5) is a comparison between DSDM and BRM.

23.2 THE PROJECT

About the Customer

Many larger European local government organizations have a special service for small businesses. The customer in this project is such a service. They provide financial help for people who run a business, or want to start a new business, if certain conditions are met. They may also decide to help independent business owners supplement their personal income. There are various financial schemes, ranging from one-off to periodic support. While funding usually takes the form of a loan, there are variations here, too. Each individual agreement is evaluated at least once a year.

The daily work is made up of many different activities: interviewing customers and candidates, matching them up with support schemes, evaluating business results, planning future steps with the customer, implementing changes in the law and in regulations. The funding involved is often a business's lifeline. Records are kept of all customer contacts and all decisions reached.

Initial Requirements and Expectations

Many of these tasks involve making legal decisions, and most of the prospective end-users were legally trained individuals. However, what this department did not want was a knowledge system that would automate the decision process. Each supported business is different, and all key decisions on funding are taken by people and not by computers.

Another thing they did not expect the new system to change was the paperwork, in the literal sense of paper documents. Many records of interviews and decisions taken (especially those taken by external agents) are still in paper form. In a few places only, the new system has replaced paper by electronic documents or database data storage.

What the customer did expect to get, however, was an application that would store the maximum information about tasks, rules and decisions in a central database, where information would no longer be replicated (single-point-of-definition). Because the work has many legal aspects, and the laws and regulations often involved change, it was important that the resulting system would be very adaptable. The new system was also expected to help users schedule their daily tasks, track the status of each case, and support the workflow between persons or services as steps or decisions were taken.

The prospective users of this particular application were mostly legal experts, a professional group already used to formulating and discussing complex and changing business rules. It was the volatility of rules and regulations involved in the work that led the customer organization to consider business rules technology.

The organization had a global, generally positive idea about DSDM before they started looking around. They chose a business rules vendor because they liked the idea of using a technology that would not only support DSDM, but also implement it directly through gradual refinement of prototypes.

Project Overview

A feasibility study that took three weeks took place in August 2000. A business study took place from October 30 to November 8, immediately followed by a functional model iteration which was concluded in the second week of 2001 (almost eight weeks, not counting holidays). At the end of this phase an interim report was produced by the team leader. The design and build phase and later activities are left outside the scope of this chapter.

The interim report was written primarily for the Executive Sponsor. Its aim was to enable the Executive Sponsor to assess the usefulness of DSDM and BRM for his/her organization and to provide a written summary of conclusions for all involved.

As for the software, the functional prototype at the end of the functional model iteration had 106 entities, 191 stated and implemented business rules, and 76 screens (60 for users, 16 for administrators). There were 340 Object Points delivered. Object Points, explained in this paper, are a measuring unit comparable to Function Points.

Each project phase was conducted according to DSDM principles. Within each phase, a business rules approach was applied throughout, from methodology to the implementation of prototypes.

23.3 BUSINESS RULES BASED METHODOLOGY

There are business rules methods and techniques for arriving at high-level or global project specifications. These we will refer to as 'business rules based methodology' (BRM).

There are also tools and practices that implement working systems using business rules specifications. They are an optional part of BRM, and can be referred to as 'business rules technology' (BRT).

Rules Repository

Administrative software systems reflect and directly support a business or part of a business: tasks people carry out, roles they play in an organization, data they enter or change, batch jobs carried out by systems, and the dependencies between all these. A central idea in BRM is that a good way of finding out how a business works and therefore how the target system should work is to unearth (capture, discover) all relevant business rules.

A business rule is anything that tells you 'how things are done' in the target business. If you work in a travel agency, you encounter such business rules as:

◆ There are Gold Card customers.

◆ Gold Card customers get a two per cent discount in peak periods.

◆ 'Adventure' Travelers must have medical insurance.

◆ Cancel or change reservations by entering a cancel date and then make a new reservation if necessary.

◆ Airline seats may not be overbooked by more than 20 per cent.

Business rules may be discovered by interviewing prospective users of the system, studying paper forms that are to be used or replaced by the new system, and generally examining the daily tasks in the business. But the most important technique to get users to talk about how things are done is to confront them with software prototypes of the target system from an early stage in the project.

Each business rule discovered is stored in a 'rules repository' in its natural language form (e.g. in English). At this point or at a later point, 'properties' of the rule are also determined. Table 23.1 lists some rule properties.

Table 23.2 is an example of a business rule from the ACUMEN repository.

It is easy to see the advantages of storing rules in a repository in this way. Here are some:

◆ Rule properties can be used as ad hoc search conditions when querying the rules. This facilitates cutting across a large rules repository in many directions.

Table 23.1 *Business Rule Properties*

Business rule property	Example values, or (in bold type) allowed values
Business area	Car rental, hotel reservations
Topic	Car fleet, car rental agreements
Task/rule set	Make reservation, cancel reservation
Priority	**'must have', 'should have', 'could have', 'won't have'**
Motivation	Billing integrity Car quality assurance Security policy Customer relationship standards International pricing
Source	Interim report document May 19 Team session November 7 Assumption Inference
Classification	Term Fact Rule Policy Objective Requirement Technical
Implementation type	**Restriction, behavior, deduction, presentation, instruction, warning, other**

Table continued on next page

Table 23.1 Continued

Business rule property	Example values, or (in bold type) allowed values
Repository version	
Search strings	
Defined (Y/N, when, by whom)	
Approved (Y/N, when, by whom)	
Implemented (Y/N, when, by whom)	
Tested (Y/N, when, by whom)	

Table 23.3 Example of Business Rules

Rule	Applicants for financial support must be over 18 years old
Business area	Financial support for independents
Topic	Applications
Task/rule set	Application take-in
Priority	Must have
Motivation	Law enforcement
Source	Team session 7 May
Classification	Rule
Implementation type	Restriction
Repository version	ACU 1.1
Search strings	Financial support, applicants, applications, age

Table continued on next page

Table 23.3 *Continued*

Rule	Applicants for financial support must be over 18 years old
Defined Y/N	Y
Defined when	10 NOV 2000
Defined by whom	JANE
Approved Y/N	Y
Approved when	14 NOV 2000
Approved by whom	RODGER
Implemented Y/N	Y
Implemented when	16 NOV 2000
Implemented by whom	JANE
Tested Y/N	N
Tested when	
Tested by whom	

◆ Management reports and team reports in natural language on what the current prototype actually claims to do ("…where implemented = 'Y' "), and what later versions are planned to do, can easily be queried from the database.

◆ Team members can work concurrently.

◆ Session notes, problem reports, change tracking, and even version control can all be appended to the rules themselves.

◆ Except when paper documents are really necessary, all project information is automatically online, single-point-of-definition, and traceable.

The single most original characteristic of rules repositories is that they do not store business logic in a procedural, linear, hierarchical way, as one is forced to do in a paper report. Rather, a rules repository is a collection of rules that individually hold true, with minimal dependencies between them. You can add, reformulate, and drop rules with minimal concern about what that means for the rest of the system. Rules are *modular* as well as *fine-grained*. You can concentrate on details of the business you are interested in, without having to worry at the same time about how to organize these details.

A second advantage of business rules is that the concept is elastic: everything about the target business that is important enough to be captured is a business rule by definition. Rules even cover essential requirements in the areas of interface design and user tasks and, more globally, business processes. In each case, you are free to concentrate on what the rule actually says, without having to determine at the same time what its conceptual status is (task, role, process, regulation, entity, property, etc.). You can optionally classify, group, and regroup rules, immediately or later, depending on project needs.

Third, BRM insists on focusing on business requirements as opposed to technical requirements. All competing methodologies also do this, including object-oriented design and workflow analysis. BRM, however, has a demonstrable affinity with business analysis as opposed to software development planning for independent, objective reasons. The information in the rules repository is in natural language form, rather than in technical terms or in diagrams. In projects such as ACUMEN, the information is stored primarily not in model diagrams or technical specifications, but in the prospective end-users' business dialects of English, French and German. BRM has a strong affinity and historical links with data modeling methods such as NIAM (more recently, FCO-IM) and ORM, which equally stress the importance of using natural language and the danger of technological bias. On the other hand, BRM is also sufficiently generic to accommodate more technology-inspired methods, such as entity/relationship and object-oriented modeling.

Rules Implementation

True business rules technology not only allows you to keep a rules repository (an excellent idea in its own right), but also to implement each rule individually, in the same modular way. If you buy a rules engine, you are entitled to expect that it keeps track of dependencies between rule implementations and that it automates runtime rules sequencing. For example, if you drop a rule and hence its implementation, the remainder of the system must still work as before.

'Rules tools' use a variety of implementation vehicles: some generate APIs or OO interfaces to databases while others generate Java classes. Most do, among many other things, what the first generation of CASE tools did: they generate a database schema from declarative specifications. In practical terms, a rule may correspond to a bit of programming code, an aspect of interface design, a database table or column, or a call to an external component, maybe a web service. Rules repositories store information about how the rules they hold are implemented.

In order to get a flavor of how rule implementations are different from event-driven implementations, consider the rule 'Gold Card customers get at least a two per cent discount':

♦ A typical event-driven implementation, where business logic is discovered primarily by examining Use Cases or doing task/role analysis, will apply this discount whenever a Gold Card customer places an order.

♦ A rules implementation will make sure that the data constellation required for this rule to hold true is always enforced, even if someone does something unforeseen to the system at runtime, such as lowering discounts of existing orders, or if some neighbouring area of the system changes at design-time in the next version of the system.

Sets of rule implementations delivered for production environments are called *rules engines*. Rules engines implement rules at each of the four logical software layers listed in Table 23.3, but they are especially good at the data and rules level, safeguarding data quality at all times. Task structures can be implemented as a subset of business rules. Sometimes a task-oriented program layer, tool, or workflow manager is used 'on top' of a rules engine.

The role of rules repositories, rule implementations, prototypes, and rules engines in BRM is summarized in Figure 23.1.

Table 23.3 *Four logical layers in software design*

Presentation, interface design
Workflow, tasks, business processes
Rules, business logic
Data structures

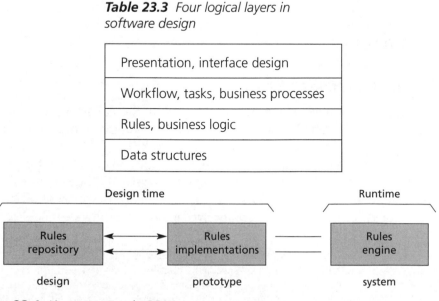

Figure 23.1 *Key concepts in BRM*

Rules engines aim to achieve the same modularity and granularity in the delivered software as in the rules discovery layer. This makes them a natural choice for step-by-step engineering or *prototyping*. You can start implementing a first prototype as soon as you have discovered about ten per cent of the business rules in a business area. The prototypes evolve to become the finished application. And this, in turn, makes BRT a natural choice for DSDM practitioners.

23.4 BUSINESS RULES IN ACUMEN

The feasibility study, the business study, and the first functional model iteration for ACUMEN were all conducted according to DSDM principles that we will not reiterate here. Instead, this section will concentrate on what it meant for these three project phases to be executed in accordance with BRM. A short evaluation will conclude this section.

BRM and Feasibility Study

In the feasibility study, the project was marked out by defining all the major areas of target functionality, as well as the commercial and organizational motivations for wanting that functionality. This resulted in a number of business area, topic, and motivation definitions in the rules repository, as well as notes recording ideas about possible solution directions. A very limited number of business rules, including presentation rules (user interface requirements), were defined and implemented. The purpose of this was to produce a first set of prototypes to make the result of the feasibility study more understandable and palatable for prospective users.

BRM and Business Study

The business study started with further detailing of the definitions marked out in the feasibility study. A first proposal for hardware, technical architecture, and tools was made. All requirements were prioritized.

Another aim of the business study was to produce an object point contract for the rest of the project. For this, an object point analysis (OPA) was required. This is comparable to function point analysis (FPA).[1] Essentially, the purpose of an OPA or FPA is to forecast the amount of work involved in building software modules.

---

[1] The reason USoft replaces FPA by OPA is that building business rules on data structures involves different cost-drivers than when you code specified system functions derived from use cases. For example, to cover a delete order function, USoft will spend considerable time getting the business rules surrounding orders right, but all current and future functions to do with Orders benefit, while conversely USoft hardly needs any time to build a 'delete screen'.

BRM is better at doing cost estimates than most other methods. At the business study stage, you do not yet have fine-grained business rule specifications in the rules repository to base cost estimates on, but you can already use the higher-level classifications in the rules repository, such as business area and topic. From previous projects, USoft has statistics on how many business rules tend to correspond to these higher-level entities, given an estimated complexity (density) of business logic. Subsequent project phases were plotted against the forecast, as shown in Figure 23.2 for the functional model iteration of ACUMEN:

In this chart, the straight horizontal line represents the estimated total number of object points for the functional model iteration. The straight diagonal line represents the estimated number of completed points per week. The assumption is made that each week an equal proportion of points will be completed. This reflects the high level of modularity and granularity in BRM projects. The wavy line represents the actual number of object points delivered each week.

BRM and Functional Model Iteration

The eight weeks of functional model iteration saw the USoft consultants build a functional prototype in close collaboration with the Advisor Users. In this phase, business rules at rules repository level played a pivotal role. They allowed a detailed

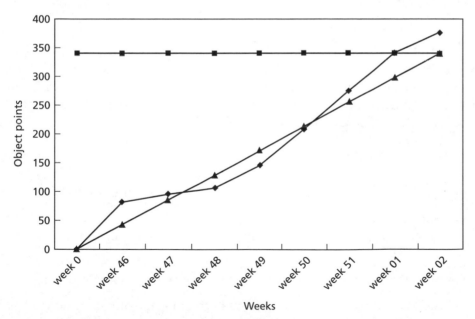

Figure 23.2 *Object points in functional model iteration of ACUMEN*

and finalized overview of all required functionality in the end-users' natural language and business dialect. Many rules reached implementation level and could be tested by prospective users. Roughly three weeks were spent producing the required database schema (tables, columns, relationships and so on), another three weeks on other business logic (data behavior, calculations, authorization), and two weeks on a first round of interface design.

Prospective users said they enjoyed the informal way of working that DSDM and BRM introduced. They were also pleased with how little paperwork they had to do. Mostly they could work directly from the prototypes. They could make notes, look up information and enter problem reports directly into the shared rules repository.

In spite of all this good news, advisor users had trouble finding out exactly how a business rule should be tested. For example, they were not sure how to test a rule such as 'Applicants for financial support must be over 18 years old'. To overcome this difficulty, a number of task definitions were introduced in the rules repository at this point, such as 'Enter new application' in the case of the example. This allowed business rules to be grouped by task and tasks to be signed off by testers.

The functional model iteration was concluded by an interim report drawn up by the team leader and primarily intended for the Executive Sponsor. One of the purposes of the report was to help the customer organization determine the value of DSDM and BRM for future projects. The report systematically discussed the nine basic DSDM principles.

Evaluation of BRM in ACUMEN

In the ACUMEN project, BRM caused problems with testing. Integrated testing was to be part of the functional model iteration phase. A form of testing was planned whereby one team member would test another member's work. This was only executed about 50 per cent of the time, putting unplanned strain on the ensuing design and build iteration phase.

Reasons for this problem were identified:

- Physical problem with missing test workstations at the planned location.

- Insufficient experience in advisor users with testing business rules implemented in software – task descriptions were used to solve this problem, as stated earlier.

- Insufficient experience in advisor users with testing software in general.

- Insufficient opportunity for members of the implementation team to support advisor users.

◆ Insufficient timeframes for advisor users to test the evolving application in addition to spending time on the facilitated workshops.

◆ The target system was planned to be 'parameterizable', in the sense that it would accommodate new types of domain entities (types of financial support to starter businesses, types of financial surveys, and so on) appearing after delivery of the system. Business rules technology of the kind facilitated by USoft is well placed to deliver this type of flexibility, but parameterization is more complex than straightforward manipulation of application data.

◆ The requirements for this particular mechanism had not crystallized until week 7 of the 8-week functional model iteration phase.

◆ Prototypes had to be fed with a certain amount of representative sample data, to be supplied by domain experts, before the mechanism was intuitive enough to be tested by advisory users.

It was noted that

◆ in this project, it would have been better if task descriptions had been introduced earlier.

◆ a possible reason for the testing problems could be that both DSDM and BRM lacked sufficient guidance on integrated testing.

◆ the problem was partly project-specific. In certain other USoft projects, testers had been perfectly comfortable with specifications in the form of business rules.

In the main, BR concepts got a warm reception from the advisor users. This may be due to a natural affinity of legal experts with business rule-based specifications. The customer organization tended to associate BRM with lower-level issues, and DSDM with the global approach, and tended to be more critical of DSDM than of BRM.

DSDM principles of empowerment and high-level requirements were among the most successfully adhered to. DSDM principles of frequent delivery and iteration were not as well understood or accepted, especially with the Executive Sponsor. The interim report therefore made an attempt to explain and justify these principles in detail. The team members representing USoft felt that too few prospective end users had been made available. More specifically, they missed Ambassador Users. In contrast, they were happy with the degree of accessibility and collaborative approach of those who did take part.

23.5 DSDM AND BUSINESS RULES

The purpose of this section is to explain why DSDM and BRM are easily combined, complementary, and of mutual benefit.

DSDM is a global approach. It is not technology specific and not even specific to projects with software deliverables.

At the 'high end' or project management level, BRM could be termed a sub-global methodology. Its central concepts are generic enough to offer general project guidelines in the same way as DSDM, and rules repositories are technology independent, but the state of the art has not taken BRM in this direction. In spite of academic support for BRM as a global methodology,[2] it is today associated with business rule implementation tools.

At the 'low end' or implementation level, BRM can go all the way to the manufacture and deployment of finished business systems, except for specialist areas. Examples of such specialist areas are internet security, graphics and artwork, electronic authentication, and specialist devices such as alarm systems. In general, BRM is highly suitable for data-intensive administrative systems, and less suitable for event-driven systems that automate or support production lines of manufacturing processes in the way robots do.

Table 23.4 lists central characteristics of the DSDM approach, namely (a) the nine basic DSDM principles, and (b) themes from other popular DSDM listings, such as the suitability filter and critical success factor listings. DSDM/BRM compatibility rating values have the following meaning:

Table 23.4 *DSDM/BRM Compatibility in Relation to Central DSDM Characteristics*

Compatibility rating	Meaning
+ +	Principle or characteristic is especially well supported by BRM.
+	Principle or characteristic is well supported by BRM.
+ –	BRM includes instruments to adhere to or enforce this principle.

---

[2] See Mallens, P.J.M. (1997) *'Business Rules-based application development'*, *Database Newsletter*, 25(3).

For business rules as the governing principle of business metadata modeling, see Date, C.J. (2000) *WHAT not HOW. The Business Rules Approach to Application Development*, Addison-Wesley.

For current academic debate in this line, see Dietz, Jan L.G. and Paul J.M. Mallens, *Business Process Modelling as a Starting Point for Information Systems Design*, Delft Technical University, Netherlands, Jan.–May 2001, published at www.brcommunity.com.

Table 23.4 Continued

Compatibility rating	Meaning
	BRM is fully compatible with this principle, but has no explicit instruments to support it.
−	BRM does nothing in particular to support or enforce this point.

DSDM principle/ critical success factor	Further explanation	DSDM/BRM compatibility	
		Rating	**Reasons**
Active user involvement		+	Non-technical concepts: rules, tasks, roles. Use of natural language at specification level. Easy prototyping
Empowerment	Teams must be put in a position to make decisions without referring back to higher levels	− −	
Frequent delivery	Delivery must take place at frequent intervals	+ +	No 'bleeding edges' in the prototype thanks to rules modularity and granularity: not everything works, but the rules that do work do so independently of neighboring unfinished edges
Fitness for business purpose	Fitness for business purpose is an essential criterion for accepting or rejecting deliverables	+	Business purposes stated in higher-level definitions within rules repository and systematically related to rule implementations
Iterative and incremental change		+ +	Granularity of rules definitions and rules implementations. Modularity of rules implementations (= automated dependency control)
Reversibility of changes		+ +	Modularity of rules implementations (= automated dependency control)

Table continued on next page

Table 23.4 *Continued*

DSDM principle/ critical success factor	Further explanation	DSDM/BRM compatibility	
		Rating	Reasons
Requirements baselined at high level	Were global requirements formulated and used later as a framework? Were these requirements sufficiently global and changeable, i.e. not too detailed or carved in stone?	+	Global categories in rules repository (Business areas, topics, motivations). Note: even detailed rule definitions are still global in the sense that they leave implementation details completely open
Instant, integrated testing		+ –	
Co-operative approach by all		+ –	
Acceptance of DSDM/BRM by target organization		– –	
Commercial commitment at high decision level	Was there a clear commercial, rather than a lower-level functional or technical, justification for the project?	+ –	
Easy access to advisor users		– –	
Stability of project team	Were the same team members present throughout the project calendar?	– –	
Knowledge and skills of project team members		– –	

Table continued on next page

***ble 23.4** Continued*

DSDM principle/ critical success factor	Further explanation	DSDM/BRM compatibility	
		Rating	Reasons
Limited size of teams	Did the size of any project teams at any one time remain under six persons?	+ −	
Prototyping-friendly technology		+ +	Easy prototyping
Demonstrable user interface in target application	Does a large part of the target application have user interfaces suitable for prototyping demonstrations?	−	
Clear ownership of target application	Is it clear who is going to own the target application?	+ −	
Modularizable functional complexity	If the target application is complex, can this complexity be broken down in manageable chunks?	+ +	Modularity of rules implementations (= automated dependency control)
Modularizable calculation complexity	If the target application contains complex calculations, can these be broken down in manageable chunks?	+ −	
Timeboxing		+ +	Granularity of rules definitions and rules implementations Modularity of rules implementations (= automated dependency control)
Prioritization of requirements		+ +	Priority property of all items in rules repository

Most items with low compatibility rating are in the area of global organization and human resource management. BRM goes a long way in supporting task assignment to team members, but it does not have instruments to optimize the assignment of persons to roles and tasks, the level of personal commitment, or the distribution of power in the organization.

23.6 CONCLUSIONS

- ◆ In the ACUMEN project, DSDM and BRM were successfully combined.

- ◆ DSDM and BRM are complementary approaches, with DSDM as a global approach and BRM as a sub-global methodology and (if required) an implementation technology.

- ◆ BRM is most supportive of DSDM in areas such as flexibility, short-term approach, prototyping, and timeboxing.

- ◆ BRM is least supportive of DSDM in the areas of human resource management, personal commitment, and distribution of power in the customer organization.

- ◆ Both with respect to DSDM and BRM, supplementary project guidelines may be needed on system testing activities.

For further information about this case study contact Rob van Haarst, NESS Benelux, www.ness-europe.com. Tel: +31 (0) 35 699 09 08. Fax. +31 (0) 35 699 09 86. E-mail: Rob.van.Haarst@ness-europe.com.

Part III

Information

Chapter 24

Where do I go From Here?

24.1 CONTACT THE DSDM CONSORTIUM

The first port of call for more information about the framework is the DSDM Consortium at www.dsdm.org. When you join as a full member you get immediate access to the online manual as well as all the UK government white papers and templates, and you can begin to use DSDM within your organization. In addition to this, you will have a wide support network of other members to refer to and receive regular updates on the latest news and events from the consortium. If you are still unsure, you can join as an associate member which will give you access to the framework on CD for evaluation purposes and access to some member areas of the website.

The active membership is the 'engine' of the consortium. It created the DSDM Framework. Any member can chair a task group to develop and evolve the framework. Ideas for framework enhancements are provided by the consortium membership. Participation in task groups by consortium members is voluntary. Task group participation can be at one of three levels: low (review only), medium (review and attend task group meetings), and high (where existing and new material is submitted for comment). The mix has turned out to be about right, with a few active contributors in each task group and many more reviewers. This has given many members the opportunity to learn from the active contributors while providing the active groups with comments based on their own practical experiences. There is nothing in the framework, the UK government white papers, and other resources that has not been suggested by or used successfully in practice by members.

For further information about the consortium and its membership and how to join, contact the DSDM secretariat at:

www.dsdm.org
info@dsdm.org

24.2 *GET TRAINED*

Because of the major cultural and process changes that come with DSDM, It is strongly recommended that formal training courses be considered. Many organizations offer general RAD and agile training, but these can often have a very different flavor from that of DSDM training. Many such courses are focused on using a particular RAD tool. By now you will have realized that agile development is far wider in its implications than the use of one or more tools.

Three forms of training are accredited by the Consortium: DSDM Aware, DSDM Practitioner, and Managing DSDM Projects. The Consortium accredits training organizations and individual courses and certifies all trainers. All accredited training is delivered by certified trainers, who have been examined by the Consortium at a level higher than that expected of those aiming for DSDM Practitioner status. Each of the courses may be followed up with an examination.

DSDM Aware is delivered in one day to all people who have an interest in the framework. These can be people such as business managers, IT managers, and project managers who are investigating whether or not DSDM is appropriate to their organization. The syllabus is general and can be understood by anyone who will potentially be involved in a DSDM project, including the users. Indeed, experience shows that an excellent way of kicking off a DSDM project is to have the whole team attend an in-house awareness training course. The result is that everyone understands their respective roles and responsibilities within the process.

The DSDM Practitioner training lasts for three days and is aimed at IT staff who will be working in a DSDM environment in whatever capacity. It covers the process and its products, the people, and the principles in more detail than is possible in the awareness day.

The two-day Managing DSDM Projects syllabus assumes that trainees will have either attended an awareness course or a practitioner course. As the name suggests, the focus is on the different approaches to project planning, monitoring, and control that come with managing empowered teams and timeboxes. The assumption is that people on the course will know about project management and simply need to learn the different approaches required in a DSDM environment.

Both the DSDM Practitioner and Managing DSDM Projects courses contain at least 50 per cent practical work, to ensure that the essential ideas covered in the courses are transmitted successfully to the trainees.

Details of accredited training providers are available on the DSDM website. Details of the examination process can be obtained from any accredited training provider or from the DSDM website (www.dsdm.org) or the British Computer Society's Information Systems Examinations Board (www.bcs.org.uk/iseb/).

24.3 A MENTOR IS ESSENTIAL

When an organization first considers using DSDM, there are many things that may have to change, even for those organizations who pride themselves on a flexible, mature, and controlled process to system development. The impact on the culture within IT and the business areas affected by DSDM projects should not be underestimated.

It is essential to get the support of someone who has experience of agile development, and DSDM in particular, to make sure that many of the common problems in introducing DSDM are either avoided or managed appropriately. Many of the problems are covered in the text of this book, but the existing culture of an organization and the personal attitudes of the staff employed in it will make some problems more likely than others.

Until your organization or someone within it has first-hand experience of DSDM, it is unlikely that everything will go as smoothly as it should. Moreover, it is difficult to believe some of the key messages of DSDM until they have been proven in an organization. Just telling people from an intellectual point of view will not be persuasive and, worse, may miss some of the important issues.

For instance, one organization made sure that they had all the infrastructure right for DSDM (including building a special room for facilitated workshops) but completely ignored the education of the development team members relating to their special responsibilities within the pilot projects. The only person who knew what the Technical Co-ordinator had to do was the Technical Co-ordinator himself. It often seemed that they did not know they *had* a Technical Co-ordinator, with the result that all the other developers ignored him. They wasted valuable effort discussing technical issues in which they were not really competent and attempting to make team decisions that really should have rested with the technical authority on the project.

Many organizations just need a few days' support from a mentor, whereas others need more significant help. The necessary level of mentoring support will depend on each individual organization. It is difficult to categorize all the different organizations, but here are some of the areas where a mentor can be very useful:

- ◆ 'Selling' the concepts of DSDM to senior business management, who need to be persuaded that this is probably the best way of getting the system they really need in the time available.

- ◆ Assessing the suitability of current working practices, procedures, and standards to the new approach. This can mean either strengthening weak controls or loosening straitjackets.

- ◆ Helping to create new working practices, procedures, and standards.

- Assisting in tool and technique selection.

- Assisting the novice DSDM project manager in putting together all aspects of the project plan.

- Providing ad hoc advice to pilot projects on request.

- Visiting pilot projects regularly (say every two weeks) to ensure that they stay on course.

- Performing 'health checks' on pilot projects on perhaps a monthly basis.

Part IV

Appendices

e-DSDM, a Specialization

FOCUSING ON THE NET

Arguably, there is no area of business where change occurs faster than in e-business. Therefore agile methods must be the first choice for developing e-business solutions. DSDM proper is a deliberately generic framework, designed to be utterly flexible in its application. E-business, though a wide area both in technical and business terms, is a relatively small sphere of project concern. Many users of DSDM found themselves approaching e-business projects and tailoring the framework to meet the particular nature of these projects. The recognition of this parallel evolution led to the formal development of e-DSDM.

e-DSDM is based on the proven DSDM framework for delivering good quality solutions that meet true business needs quickly and effectively. It is usable for all categories of e-business where internet, intranet, or extranet-based systems are being developed: it is applicable to business-to-business, business-to-customer, and business-to-worker projects.

As an organization's e-business capability grows from simple 'brochureware' to web-based solutions that support transactional processing, the impact is felt by a wider cross-section of the organization. Areas such as marketing, finance, customer service, manufacturing, product development, distribution, and IT will have an interest in the solution. e-DSDM has been designed to ensure that the needs of all these stakeholders are addressed.

All the basic roles in DSDM are carried over into e-DSDM, many of them with some alteration, For instance, in a B2C environment, it is important that a number of Advisor Users are identified who have the characteristic skills of prospective customers, so that for each iteration a new set of Advisor Users come to the prototype with no preconceived ideas as to how the product will operate. Several new roles specific to e-DSDM have been introduced, such as the Content Manager, the

Marketing Representative, the Web Designer, and the Webmaster. Alongside these new roles the nature of e-business projects requires new products within the development. These include the Interaction Design, Security Policy, Technical Architecture Prototype, and the User Involvement Strategy (see note on Advisor Users above, for an indication of what this product does).

As well as changes to the specifics of the lifecycle, roles, and products of DSDM, e-DSDM recognizes the potential damage that a poor website can do to any organization. Extensive checklists are supplied to assist development projects in focusing on those aspects of IT and business change that are crucial to successful e-business sites, such as security and usability of the site once it is in use.

e-DSDM categorizes projects according to the e-business 'audience' (customers, other businesses or the workforce) and the type of project being undertaken within an e-business program (from providing simple information to creating a system which is integrated with enterprise systems). For each category, e-DSDM defines an optimum path through the process highlighting what is important, what can be omitted with safety, and where any special considerations lie.

The Agile Manifesto

Facilitating change is more effective than attempting to prevent it. Learn to trust in your ability to respond to unpredictable events; it's more important than trusting in your ability to plan for disaster.

by Martin Fowler *and* Jim Highsmith

This article was first published in *Software Development*, August 2001.

In the past 12–18 months, a wide range of publications – *Software Development, IEEE Software, Cutter IT Journal, Software Testing and Quality Engineering,* and even *The Economist* – have published articles on what Martin Fowler calls the 'New Methodology' reflecting a growing interest in these new approaches to software development (Extreme Programming, Crystal Methodologies, SCRUM, Adaptive Software Development, Feature-Driven Development and DSDM among them). In addition to these 'named' methodologies, scores of organizations have developed their own 'lighter' approach to building software.

Formation of the Agile Alliance

On 11–13 February, 2001, at The Lodge at Snowbird ski resort in the Wasatch mountains of Utah, 17 people met to talk, ski, relax and try to find common ground. What emerged was the Agile Software Development Alliance.

A bigger gathering of organizational anarchists would be hard to find, so what emerged from this meeting was symbolic – a *Manifesto for Agile Software Development*, signed by all participants. Although the Manifesto provides some specifics, a deeper theme drives many Alliance members. At the close of the two-day meeting, Extreme Programming mentor Bob Martin joked that he was about to make a 'mushy' statement. Though tinged with humour, Bob's sentiments were shared by the group – we all enjoyed working with people who shared compatible goals and values based on mutual trust and respect, promoting collaborative, people-focused organizational models, and building the types of professional communities in which we would want to work.

The agile methodology movement is not anti-methodology; in fact, many of us want to restore credibility to the word. We also want to restore a balance: we embrace modelling, but not merely to file some diagram in a dusty corporate repository. We embrace documentation, but not to waste reams of paper in never-maintained and rarely-used tomes. We plan, but recognize the limits of planning in a turbulent environment. Those who brand proponents of XP, SCRUM or any of the other agile methodologies as 'hackers' are ignorant of both the methodologies and the original definition of the term (a 'hacker' was first defined as a programmer who enjoys solving complex programming problems, rather than someone who practices ad hoc development or destruction).

Early on, Alistair Cockburn identified the general disgruntlement with the word *light*: 'I don't mind the methodology being called light in weight, but I'm not sure I want to be referred to as a "lightweight" attending a "lightweight methodologists" meeting. It sounds like a bunch of skinny, feebleminded people trying to remember what day it is.' So our first task was to come up with a new adjective that we could live with. Now our processes are 'agile', even if some of us are a bit creaky.

The result of this meeting (and the ensuing frenzied online interaction) was the Agile Manifesto. While the purpose and principles of the Manifesto were developed by the entire group, we (Jim and Martin, both authors of the Manifesto) have added, for this article, our own interpretations and explanations.

The Agile Manifesto: Purpose

'We are uncovering better ways of developing software by doing it and helping others do it. We value:

◆ Individuals and interactions over processes and tools.

◆ Working software over comprehensive documentation.

◆ Customer collaboration over contract negotiation.

◆ Responding to change over following a plan.'

This statement has a number of fascinating aspects, not least of which was getting 17 people to agree to it. First, the word *uncovering*. While this was a group of experienced and recognized software development 'gurus', the word *uncovering* was selected to assure (or frighten) the audience that the Alliance members don't have all the answers and don't subscribe to the silver-bullet theory.

Second, the phrase *by doing it* indicates that the members actually practise these methods in their own work. Ken Schwaber (a proponent of SCRUM) told of his days of selling tools to automate comprehensive, 'heavy' methodologies. Impressed by the responsiveness of Ken's company, Jeff Sutherland (SCRUM) asked him which of these heavy methodologies he used internally for development. 'I still remember the look on Jeff's face,' Ken remarked, 'when I told him, "None – if we used any of them, we'd be out of business!"'

Third, this group is about helping, not telling. The Alliance members want to help others with agile methods, and to further our own knowledge by learning from those we try to help.

The value statements have a form: In each bullet point, the first segment indicates a preference, while the latter segment describes an item that, though important, is of lesser priority. This distinction lies at the heart of agility, but simply asking people to list what's valuable doesn't flesh out essential differences. Roy Singham, Martin's boss at ThoughtWorks, put it well when he said that it's the edge cases, the hard choices, that interest him. 'Yes, we value planning, comprehensive documentation, processes and tools. That's easy to say. The hard thing is to ask "what do you value *more*?"'

The Alliance recognizes the importance of process and tools, with the additional recognition that the interaction of skilled individuals is of even greater importance. Similarly, comprehensive documentation is not necessarily bad, but the primary focus must remain on the final product – delivering working software. Therefore, every project team needs to determine for itself what documentation is absolutely essential.

Contract negotiation, whether through an internal project charter or external legal contract, isn't a bad practice, just an insufficient one. Contracts and project charters may provide some boundary conditions within which the parties can work, but only through on-going collaboration can a development team hope to understand and deliver what the client wants.

No one can argue that following a plan is a good idea – right? Well, yes and no. In the turbulent world of business and technology, scrupulously following a plan can have dire consequences, even if it's executed faithfully. However carefully a plan is crafted, it becomes dangerous if it blinds you to change. We've examined plenty of successful projects and few, if any, delivered what was planned in the beginning, yet they succeeded because the development team was agile enough to respond again and again to external changes.

The Agile Manifesto: Principles

Our highest priority is to satisfy the customer through early and continuous delivery of valuable software.

In a recent workshop, a software development manager questioned the feature or story approach to iterative cycle planning. 'But aren't requirements specifications and architecture documents important?' he asked. 'Yes,' Jim replied, 'They *are* important, but we need to understand that customers don't care about documents, UML diagrams or legacy integration. Customers care about whether or not you're delivering working software to them every development cycle – some piece of business functionality that proves to them that the evolving software application serves their business needs.'

Implementing a 'customer value' principle is one of those 'easier said than done' activities. Traditional project management practices assume that achieving a plan equals project success equals demonstrated customer value. The volatility associated with today's projects demands that customer value be re-evaluated frequently, and meeting original project plans may not have much bearing on a project's ultimate success.

> Welcome changing requirements, even late in development. Agile processes harness change for the customer's competitive advantage.

The growing unpredictability of the future is one of the most challenging aspects of the new economy. Turbulence – in both business and technology – causes change, which can be viewed either as a threat to be guarded against or as an opportunity to be embraced.

Rather than resist change, the agile approach strives to accommodate it as easily and efficiently as possible, while maintaining an awareness of its consequences. Although most people agree that feedback is important, they often ignore the fact that the result of accepted feedback is change. Agile methodologies harness this result, because their proponents understand that facilitating change is more effective than attempting to prevent it.

> Deliver working software frequently, from a couple of weeks to a couple of months, with a preference for the shorter timescale.

For many years, process gurus have been telling everyone to use an incremental or iterative style of software development, with multiple deliveries of ever-growing functionality. While the practice has grown in use, it's still not predominant; however, it's essential for agile projects. Furthermore, we push hard to reduce delivery cycle time.

However, remember that *deliver* is not the same as *release*. The business people may have valid reasons for not putting code into production every couple of weeks. We've seen projects that haven't achieved releasable functionality for a year or more. But that doesn't exempt them from the rapid cycle of internal deliveries that allows everyone to evaluate and learn from the growing product.

Business people and developers work together daily throughout the project.

Many folks want to buy software the way they buy a car. They have a list of features in mind, they negotiate a price, and they pay for what they asked for. This simple buying model is appealing, but for most software projects, it doesn't work. So agile developers respond with a radical change in our concept of the requirements process.

For a start, we don't expect a detailed set of requirements to be signed off at the beginning of the project; rather, we see a high-level view of requirements that is subject to frequent change. Clearly, this is not enough to design and code, so the gap is closed with frequent interaction between the business people and the developers. The frequency of this contact often surprises people. We put 'daily' in the principle to emphasize the software customer's continuing commitment to actively take part in, and indeed take joint responsibility for, the software project.

Build projects around motivated individuals, give them the environment and support they need and trust them to get the job done.

Deploy all the tools, technologies and processes you like, even our agile processes, but in the end, it's people who make the difference between success and failure. We realize that however hard we work in coming up with process ideas, the best we can hope for is a second-order effect on a project. So it's important to maximize that first-order people factor.

For many people, trust is the hardest thing to give. Decisions must be made by the people who know the most about the situation. This means that managers must trust their staff to make the decisions about the things they're paid to know about.

The most efficient and effective method of conveying information with and within a development team is face-to-face conversation.

Inevitably, when discussing agile methodologies, the topic of documentation arises. Our opponents appear apoplectic at times, deriding our 'lack' of documentation. It's enough to make us scream, 'the issue is *not* documentation – the issue is *understanding*!' Yes, physical documentation has heft and substance, but the real measure of success is abstract: Will the people involved gain the understanding they need? Many of us are writers, but despite our awards and book sales, we know that writing is a difficult and inefficient communication medium. We use it because we have to, but most project teams can and should use more direct communication techniques.

'Tacit knowledge cannot be transferred by getting it out of people's heads and onto paper,' writes Nancy Dixon in *Common Knowledge* (Harvard Business School Press, 2000). 'Tacit knowledge can be transferred by moving the people who have the knowledge around. The reason is that tacit knowledge is not only the facts but the relationships among the facts – that is, how people might combine certain facts to deal with a specific situation.' So the distinction between agile and document-centric methodologies is not one of extensive documentation versus no documentation; rather a differing concept of the blend of documentation and conversation required to elicit understanding.

Working software is the primary measure of progress.

Too often, we've seen project teams who don't realize they're in trouble until a short time before delivery. They met the requirements on time, the design on time, maybe even the code on time, but testing and integration took much longer than they thought. We favour iterative development primarily because it provides milestones that can't be fudged, which imparts an accurate measure of the progress and a deeper understanding of the risks involved in any given project. As Chet Hendrickson, co-author of *Extreme Programming Installed* (Addison-Wesley, 2000), remarks, 'If a project is going to fail, I'd rather know that after one month than after 15.'

Working software is the measure of progress because there's no other way of capturing the subtleties of the requirements: documents and diagrams are too abstract to let the user "kick the tires," says Dave Thomas, coauthor of *The Pragmatic Programmer* (Addison-Wesley, 1999).

Agile processes promote sustainable development. The sponsors, developers and users should be able to maintain a constant pace indefinitely.

Our industry is characterized by long nights and weekends, during which people try to undo the errors of unresponsive planning. Ironically, these long hours don't actually lead to greater productivity. Martin and Kent Beck have often recalled working at companies where they spent all day removing errors made late the previous night.

Agility relies upon people who are alert and creative, and can maintain that alertness and creativity for the full length of a software development project. Sustainable development means finding a working pace (40 or so hours a week) that the team can sustain over time and remain healthy.

Continuous attention to technical excellence and good design enhances agility.

When many people look at agile development, they see reminders of the 'quick and dirty' RAD (Rapid Application Development) efforts of the last decade. But, while agile development is similar to RAD in terms of speed and flexibility, there's a big difference when it comes to technical cleanliness. Agile approaches emphasize quality of design, because design quality is essential to maintaining agility.

One of the tricky aspects, however, is the fact that agile processes assume and encourage the alteration of requirements while the code is being written. As such, design cannot be a purely up-front activity to be completed before construction. Instead, design is a continuous activity that's performed throughout the project. Each and every iteration will have design work.

The different agile processes emphasize different design styles. FDD has an explicit step at the beginning of each iteration in which design is executed, usually graphically with the UML. XP places great emphasis on refactoring to allow the design to evolve as development proceeds. But all of these processes borrow from each other: FDD uses refactoring as developers revisit earlier design decisions, and XP encourages short design sessions before coding tasks. In all cases, the project's design is enhanced continually throughout the project.

Simplicity – the art of maximizing the amount of work not done – is essential.

Any software development task can be approached with a host of methods. In an agile project, it's particularly important to use simple approaches, because they're easier to change. It's easier to add something to a process that's too simple than it is to take something away from a process that's too complicated. Hence, there's a strong taste of minimalism in all the agile methods. Include only what everybody needs rather than what anybody needs, to make it easier for teams to add something that addresses their own particular needs.

'Simple, clear purpose and principles give rise to complex, intelligent behaviour,' says Dee Hock, former CEO of Visa International. 'Complex rules and regulations give rise to simple, stupid behaviour.' No methodology can ever address all the complexity of a modern software project. Giving people a simple set of rules and encouraging their creativity will produce far better outcomes than imposing complex, rigid regulations.

The best architectures, requirements and designs emerge from self-organizing teams.

Contrary to what you've heard, form doesn't follow function: form follows failure. 'The form of made things is always subject to change in response to their real or perceived shortcomings, their failures to function properly,' writes Henry Petroski, civil engineering professor and author of *The Evolution of Useful Things* (Vintage Books, 1994). Stuart Brand writes that the 'form follows function' idea has misled architects into believing that they could predict how buildings would actually be used.

Petroski's views are similar to one of the two key points of this principle – that the best designs (architectures, requirements) emerge from iterative development and use rather than from early plans. The second point of the principle is that emergent properties (*emergence*, a key property of complex systems, roughly translates to innovation and creativity in human organizations) are best generated from self-organizing teams in which the interactions are high and the process rules are few.

At regular intervals, the team reflects on how to become more effective, then tunes and adjusts its behaviour accordingly.

Agile methods are not something you pick and follow slavishly. You may start with one of these processes, but we all recognize that we can't come up with the right process for every situation. So any agile team must refine and reflect as it goes along, constantly improving its practices in its local circumstances.

Jim has been working with a consulting company to develop an Adaptive Software Development–Extreme Programming combination methodology. The first team to use it modified it immediately. Martin has worked with a number of teams at ThoughtWorks to tailor Extreme Programming practices to various project situations. Trust in people, believing that individual capability and group interaction are key to success extends to trusting teams to monitor and improve their own development processes.

Toward an Agile Future

Early response to the Agile Manifesto has been gratifying. Several e-mails expressed sentiments such as, 'My product manager has already posted the Manifesto on her wall.' Many of Martin's colleagues at ThoughtWorks have popped in to say how much they shared the values.

One question that arose immediately was whether or not the Alliance was a precursor to what one conference attendee tagged a 'Unified Lightweight Methodology'. Absolutely not! While the group believes that a set of common purposes and principles will benefit the users of agile methodologies, we are equally adamant that variety and diversity of practices are necessary. When it comes to methodologies, each project is different and each project team is different – there's no one-size-fits-all solution.

What of the future? We can confidently say that we don't know. Agility is all about trusting in one's ability to respond to unpredictable events more than trusting in one's ability to plan ahead for them. We also know that the personal relationships formed by our collaboration matter far more than the document that we've produced. One thing is clear: we've only just started.

THE MANIFESTO FOR AGILE SOFTWARE DEVELOPMENT

Seventeen anarchists agree:

We are uncovering better ways of developing software by doing it and helping others do it. Through this work we have come to value:

Individuals and interactions over processes and tools.

Working software over comprehensive documentation.

Customer collaboration over contract negotiation.

Responding to change over following a plan.

That is, while we value the items on the right, we value the items on the left more. We follow the following principles:

◆ Our highest priority is to satisfy the customer through early and continuous delivery of valuable software.

◆ Welcome changing requirements, even late in development. Agile processes harness change for the customer's competitive advantage.

◆ Deliver working software frequently, from a couple of weeks to a couple of months, with a preference to the shorter timescale.

◆ Business people and developers work together daily throughout the project.

◆ Build projects around motivated individuals. Give them the environment and support they need, and trust them to get the job done.

◆ The most efficient and effective method of conveying information to and within a development team is face-to-face conversation.

◆ Working software is the primary measure of progress.

◆ Agile processes promote sustainable development. The sponsors, developers and users should be able to maintain a constant pace indefinitely.

◆ Continuous attention to technical excellence and good design enhances agility.

◆ Simplicity – the art of maximizing the amount of work not done – is essential.

◆ The best architectures, requirements and designs emerge from self-organizing teams.

◆ At regular intervals, the team reflects on how to become more effective, then tunes and adjusts its behaviour accordingly.

Kent Beck, Mike Beedle, Arie van Bennekum, Alistair Cockburn, Ward Cunningham, Martin Fowler, James Grenning, Jim Highsmith, Andrew Hunt, Ron Jeffries, Jon Kern, Brian Marick, Robert C. Martin, Steve Mellor, Ken Schwaber, Jeff Sutherland, Dave Thomas.

Published by permission of *Software Development*.

References

Framework for Business Centred Development, Version 4.1, obtainable from the DSDM Consortium.

Dynamic Systems Development Method and TickIT, ISBN 0-580-27081-5.

Beck, Kent (2000) *Extreme Programming Explained*, Addison-Wesley. ISBN 0-201-61641-6.

Boehm, Barry (1998) 'A Spiral Model for Software Development and Enhancement', *Computer*, 21(5), May.

Brooks, Frederick P. (1975) *The Mythical Man-Month*, Addison-Wesley. ISBN 0-201-00650-2.

Martin, James (1991) *Rapid Application Development*, Macmillan. ISBN 0-02-376775-8.

Rush, Gary (1985) 'The fast way to define system requirements', *In Depth*, *Computerworld*, 7 October.

SUGGESTIONS FOR FURTHER READING

Cockburn, Alistair (2001) *Agile Software Development*, Addison-Wesley. ISBN 0-201-69969-9.

Folkes, Susan, and Stubenvoll, Sue (1992) *Accelerated Systems Development*, Prentice Hall. ISBN 0-13-006073-9.

Gottesdiener, Ellen (2002) *Requirements by Collaboration*, Addison-Wesley. ISBN 0-201-78606-0.

Highsmith, Jim (2000) 'Adaptive Software Development', Dorset House. ISBN 0-932-63340-4.

McConnell, Steve (1996) *Rapid Development: Taming Wild Software Schedules*, Microsoft Press. ISBN 1-55615-900-5.

Index

Coventry University